Revealing Islam

and

Its Role In

The End Times

Robert Keeton, D. RE., Th.D.

Copyright 2014

II TIMOTHY 3:5

Having a form of godliness, but denying the power thereof: from such turn away.

First printing June 2014

Copyright ©2014
By Robert Keeton and Rock of Ages Ministries

All Bible quotations are from the
King James Version

All Qur'an quotations are from the
Abdullah Yusif Ali English translation
New revised 5th edition 1989

For information write:
Rock of Ages Ministries
P.O. Box 2308
Cleveland, TN. 37320
or visit:
www.roapm.com

Printed By: Rock of Ages Ministries
in the United States of America

ISBN-978-0-9903494-0-2

Biographical Sketch of the Author

Robert Bryan Keeton was born September 25, 1954, in Monticello, Kentucky, and at the age of one his family moved to Elkton, Kentucky where he grew up on his parent's farm. He was the tenth of twelve children born to James Bryan and Clasteen Keeton.

He attended public school, and graduated from Todd County Central High School in 1972. He then moved to Indiana where he met his wife-to-be Deborah Kay Trivett. They were married December 3, 1973. They have two children Bryan Edward Keeton and Tonya Kay Keeton Shelby and six grandchildren.

On December 10, 1981, at the age of 27 he was saved, in his home after studying a chapter with his wife, from a booklet entitled "After Salvation." The booklet was one that the Rock of Ages Prison Ministry handed out to those incarcerated in prisons all across America. Ironically, this is the ministry in which he would later serve the Lord.

Two years later God began to deal with his heart to preach. God continued to deal with his heart for nearly three more years, and on August 19, 1986, he surrendered to preach God's Word.

Robert owned and operated his own business and had as many as eight crews working for him during this time. As time passed, God began to open doors of opportunity for him to preach in nursing homes and churches. The responsibilities of the business that he once loved became more of a burden because of the call of

God upon his life.   He was open to any opportunities God allowed.

In April 1987, he agreed to go on a prison revival that Dr. Ron Gearis had invited him to go to as a volunteer with the Rock of Ages Prison Ministry. The revival was at the Parchman State Prison in Clarksdale, Mississippi. It was there that God broke his heart for the spiritual need he saw among the prisoners. After returning from the prison revival, on April 10, 1987, God confirmed through His Word *(To give light to them that sit in darkness and in the shadow of death, to guide our feet into the way of peace. Luke 1:79)* that the Rock of Ages Prison Ministry was where God wanted him to serve as a missionary.

On April 14, 1987 the Board of Directors met and interviewed Robert and his family, and they were accepted that day as missionaries. He was ordained and sent out from his church on August 16, 1987.

Robert and his family stepped out by faith to serve the Lord in the call that God had placed upon their lives. For the next eleven and one half years their home would be mobile in a Fifth Wheel Recreational Vehicle (RV) to accomplish taking the Word of God to the prisoners. They traveled from prison to prison as God opened opportunities for them to do so. They are no longer in the RV but now reside in Cleveland, Tennessee, where they continue to serve with the Rock of Ages Prison Ministry.

Robert has served the Lord in the Rock of Ages Prison Ministry in many positions such as: Revival Team member, Revival Team Coordinator, International (Foreign) Team Coordinator, Director of Training, Executive Director of Rock of Ages College of Biblical Studies, and is presently serving as the Director of Education.

His present position has him directing or overseeing the training of all Rock of Ages Ministries Missionaries and volunteers for prison, military, and the public school ministry. He is also over the Rock of Ages College of Biblical Studies and Theological Seminary with over 230 external study students. Another department under his supervision is the Discipleship Institute, which is also a Bible Study program by correspondence made available to the prisoners, church members, school students, and military personnel. Presently there are approximately 24,000 students (in eight countries) studying God's Word through this program.

Robert has earned a Bachelor of Divinity, Masters in Religious Education from Great Plains Baptist College, a Doctor of Religious Education from American Baptist College, and a Doctor of Theology from Rock of Ages Theological Seminary.

Presently Robert serves as a member of the Executive Staff and a member of the Board of Directors of the Rock of Ages Ministries.

Robert has been educating missionaries concerning the religion of Islam from January 1996 to present day. He has also conducted informational seminars in several churches on the subject of Islam and their connections with the end times or last days. God has burdened his heart to equip the children of God not only to know about but to know how to deal with this religion.

Dedication and Acknowledgement

I would like to dedicate this writing to the late Dr. Ronald Gearis, President of the Rock of Ages Prison Ministry (1987 – 2006). He was the one that made the initial decision for me to do this study and implement it as part of the training program for the Rock of Ages Prison Ministry. It was in May 1995 that Dr. Gearis looked at me and said, "I want a course to train our missionaries how to deal with the Muslims in the prisons."

I had no desire to study this subject because of the conflicts that I and other Rock of Ages missionaries were having in the prisons with Muslims. It was Dr. Gearis that saw the great need for this material when we were just beginning our training program to prepare our missionaries for service in the prisons. This was the first course that he wanted developed.

My initial goal was to begin to minimize and finally end any Muslim intrusions in our efforts to witness to the other prisoners. They had, in a sense, become a thorn in the flesh of our efforts in the prisons because they were becoming such a hindrance to the revival teams when we entered the prisons. They were becoming more and more confrontational and volatile. No longer were they waiting for us to come to their cell or by their bunk, they were now approaching us. Their purpose was to stop us from giving the Gospel to anyone they might be trying to convert to their religious beliefs. There always seemed to be a spokesperson and several listeners. The spokesperson would always ask questions about Bible passages that they thought were contradictions, or that they thought supported their Qur'an and its teachings. They were always attempting to try to make the Christian look ignorant or unprepared.

Then God began to break my heart for them, and to remind me that Christ also died for them. The focus then became to remove the rubbish that was in the way so that we could begin to build. Much like the rebuilding of the walls of Jerusalem, they had to get rid of the rubbish before they could build. This is the approach that God has shown me.

This approach has been put into practice as I have entered the prisons, and I have had the privilege of leading many Muslims to Christ for God's glory. The training has also equipped many of our missionaries to deal with the Muslims much more effectively than they were able to before.

Again, a special thanks to Dr. Gearis for challenging me to do this work so that we might see Muslims saved by the blood of our Lord Jesus Christ.

Also, a special thanks to my wife Debbie, for enduring the many long hours of study, writing, and rewriting to complete this work. She has been a great encouragement to me to keep on keeping on. She has sacrificed and allowed me to invest literally hundreds and hundreds of hours in this work that we might see Muslims come to know Christ as their Saviour too.

PREFACE

The purpose of this course was originally to help the missionaries of the Rock of Ages Prison Ministry. However, since the completion of this study course, that view has been greatly enlarged. It is much more needed today than it was in earlier times.

The religion of Islam is rapidly spreading around the world. Its presence has not just recently appeared nor have its teachings just come upon the scene. It is one of the oldest religions in the world today dating back historically to approximately A.D. 610.

The teachings of Islam are directly opposed to those of Christianity and the very things upon which Christianity is founded. Islam uses only the parts of the Bible that suits its purpose and then vehemently denies the rest using the excuse that man has rewritten and changed the Bible to suit his own desires.

Within the prisons of our country, as well as many other countries, the Muslim presence is becoming very prevalent. Some of the followers of Islam, especially in our American prisons, are more racist and radical than religious. In the prisons here in the United States, Islam has become more of a means of identification, protection, and power than anything else. Concerning those just mentioned, there is not much hope of dealing with them using the Christian's normal approach, even though one may occasionally get saved. To see one of these saved is truly exceptional.

I hope that the information contained herein will be a great help to you as we endeavor to look at what Muslims believe, but even more at how they might be dealt with effectively to bring them to a saving knowledge of Jesus Christ.

All Christians do not fit the same description or mold and neither do Muslims. I hope you will understand that not all the information that is in this material will fit every Muslim. However, they are using the same book as their authority; the Qur'an is their guide, and they are to abide by it as the authority in all matters.

I will share first the basic beliefs and practices of the Islamic faith, then we will also look at how to win them to Christ, and finally their role in the end times.

The more we know about what they believe and their history or background, the more chance there will be to reach them and deal with them more effectively from the Word of God.

In December 1995, USA Today published statistics stating that for the first time in the history of the United States, blacks (African Americans) now make up a majority of the prison population.

This means that now the majority of our congregations in the prisons, and the ones we are going to be dealing with in the prison housing units will be African American. Blacks are definitely the target of the Muslims in the prisons of America.

Therefore we are going to be in competition with Muslims to see who will convert them first. This is not meant to be a racial statement, but it is based on statistical facts. This is the reason they have become and will continue to be more and more aggressive toward any Christian ministry as we enter the prisons. They see us as an enemy or opposition invading their territory where they are trying to influence others toward their beliefs.

USA Today also published another article around the same time frame of December 1995, stating that in the prisons of South Carolina, pork is no longer an option on the prison menu. I state this to show the influence that Muslims are having even within the prison system.

This is just a sample of the influence the Islamic community is now having in the prison system. They have played a major role in stopping Christian groups from going into the housing areas of many prisons to witness; because they have complained that it is an invasion of their privacy.

For years our ministry has been hearing statements and reports such as: "When you all leave we see a difference in the atmosphere and attitudes of the inmates." "When you come it makes a difference that we can see." "We look forward to you all coming." "You all help to relieve a lot of pressures in the prison."

The Muslims will complain and do all they can to stop us from coming into the prisons. They will try to coerce you into a heated argument so the officers will blame the Christian for causing the disturbances and disruptions. What conclusion do you think the officers and prison officials will come to? The Christian groups are to blame. The prison's solution, eliminate the cause, "Christian groups going in the housing units, or even into the prison."

The same approach that I teach our missionaries to use inside the prisons with those that are turning to Islam is the approach that works outside the prison too. It is a way of reaching those that God has put in our paths.

Proverbs 24:6
For by wise counsel
thou shalt make thy war:

TABLE OF CONTENTS

Biographical Sketch Of The Author...i
Dedication And Acknowledgement..iv
Preface...vi
Introduction...1
Chapter I
The Strategy To Reach The Muslim..11
Chapter II
Our Knowledge Of The Religion Of Islam..................................24
Chapter III
History Of Islam...31
Chapter IV
A Brief Look At Some Of Islam's Basic Belief............................57
Chapter V
Divisions Or Branches Of Islam..66
Chapter VI
The Five Doctrinal Pillars Of Islam..77
Chapter VII
Religious Practices Of Islam...84
Chapter VIII
Prophets Of Islam...89
Chapter IX
The Koran (Qur'an) Of Islam...119
Chapter X
The God (Allah) Of Islam...130
Chapter XI
The Angels Of Islam..142
Chapter XII
The Last Days And Salvation...150
Chapter XIII
Islam's View Of Creation..164
Chapter XIV
Koran (Qur'an) References To Use..183
Chapter XV
Islam's Role In End Times..197
Chapter XVI
Islam's Role In Tribulation Times...211
Bibliography..223

Revealing Islam
and
Its Role In The End Times

Introduction

I Corinthians 12:31 But covet earnestly the best gifts: and yet shew I unto you a more excellent way.

In I Corinthians 12:31, the apostle Paul wrote to the church at Corinth and to us that the Word of God declares the more excellent way. Not just a way but a more excellent way. We often hear people proclaim that there is more than one way to Christ.

Proverbs 16:25 There is a way that seemeth right unto a man, but the end thereof are the ways of death.

Oh, there are other ways, but they lead to the way of death, not unto life, forgiveness of sin, and eternal life with Christ in heaven. These other ways are only deceptions of the devil, who John 8:44 says is the father of all who have not received Christ as their Saviour.

John 14:6 Jesus saith unto him, I am the way, the truth, and the life: no man cometh unto the Father, but by me.

Jesus is the only way according to the Bible. The Bible is the

1

only book that we recognize as the inspired, preserved, inerrant, infallible Word of God. The Bible has always been the authority even before the Qur'an came into existence. In this book of authority, Jesus, who is the very Word of God, even declared himself to be "The Way." Jesus did so, not just as an optional choice, for entrance into heaven, but as the only way into heaven. However, you will quickly find when talking with a Muslim that Jesus is not accepted as "The Way," as He has declared Himself in the above verse to be. Later we will see that Jesus is even called "The Way" in the Qur'an, but they still deny Him as "The Way."

The Word of God gives an ample description of the religion of Islam, its followers, its beliefs, and what we should do concerning these in II Timothy 3:5.

> *II Timothy 3:5 Having a form of godliness, but denying the power thereof: from such turn away.*

Even with the warning straight from the Word of God, multitudes are flocking to this religion, that denies Jesus Christ as The Way, the Son of God, God in the flesh, Saviour of the world, and the Hope of Glory, and many, many other things.

Jesus in His own words even warned us of the things that are now coming to pass, such as the violence of Muslims towards the Jews and Christians.

> *John 16:1-3 These things have I spoken unto you, that ye should not be offended.*
> *2 They shall put you out of the synagogues: yea, the time cometh, that whosoever killeth you will think that he doeth God service.*
> *3 And these things will they do unto you, because they have not known the Father, nor me.*

The purpose of this writing is twofold. First, we need to make people aware of the religion of Islam and the dangers that it imposes upon the world. Secondly, we need to encourage and equip God's people to carry out the Great Commission with needed information and a way to reach Muslims with the Gospel.

Since the disaster of September 11, 2001, the interest of non-Muslims around the world to learn about this religion that has been linked to this attack has increased as never before.

Since the attacks on the twin towers in New York, people have been buying all the books they can about this religion to get insight and understanding, and there have since been multitudes of books written about Islam.

These books all tell of their practices, beliefs and statistics. However, I have yet to see one that really equips the child of God with knowledge of how to deal with a follower of Islam. As I studied and prepared this material to train our missionaries, I purchased and read many of these books, only to find that they repeated each other. They never really gave any information that would give insight as to how to get the Muslim to listen to what the Bible had to say. Since Muslims believe the Bible is and has been corrupted and is not a valid source of authority, this was a major issue to me. The question that kept coming to my mind was "why was no one leading or equipping God's people in the right direction to win Muslims to Christ?"

A majority of these books are written by supposedly, "former Muslims" that have put their trust in Christ. I would think that it should be "former Muslims" that would know more than anyone else the most effective way to reach a Muslim. They know that Muslims do not believe the Bible to be the Word of God. Now, my question is, are they not telling us "the most effective way" because they are not really saved? Do they intentionally want to

3

mislead us so we will not be able to win Muslims to Christ? I am not saying every single one of them, but many of them perhaps. The Word of God declares that we will know them by their fruits. Are they producing fruit themselves evidenced by other Muslims coming to Christ? Are they really equipping Christians with the knowledge to win Muslims to Christ? Are they really expressing a burden to reach their people with the Gospel? I believe the majority of these so-called former Muslims are not doing these things we just brought into question, which should be of utmost importance if they are saved.

Information gained from my studies and from reports concerning the actions of the Muslim pilots that flew the planes into the towers on September 11, 2001, revealed some interesting facts. Apparently they are permitted to do things that the Qur'an and their religion strictly forbid if it will mislead the infidels (non-Muslims) or their enemies and gain victory for Allah. With this in mind, is it possible that many of these books then are written by Muslims and not former Muslims in an attempt to mislead God's people, so that we will not be effective in witnessing to a Muslim?

In my studies I found that there are at least four situations when it is permissible for a Muslim to lie according to their teachings. First, a husband can lie in his marriage concerning his faithfulness. Second, a Muslim can lie to his enemies in order to deceive them so that they will be defeated. Third, a Muslim can even lie to another Muslim in order to reconcile. Finally, a Muslim can lie if he or his god will benefit from it.

I started in May of 1995 studying and preparing materials on the religion of Islam and continue to do so at this present time. Since January 1996, I have been teaching those things that I have gleaned on the religion of Islam, in an attempt to prepare our missionaries to be able to deal with them and to win them to Christ. I have invested literally hundreds and hundreds of hours in studying Islamic religion and its followers. The more I learn of this religion, the more I am amazed that people would follow such a belief system at all; and how they reject Christ for who He really is amazes me even more. However, I should expect them to reject Christ according to what the Bible says.

> *II Corinthians 4:4 In whom the god of this world hath blinded the minds of them which believe not, lest the light of the glorious gospel of Christ, who is the image of God, should shine unto them.*

In days following September 11, 2001, I received emails and written materials from many people who knew I had been studying Islam. The following is from an insert in a church bulletin just as it was written, entitled "Something to Think About."

SOMETHING TO THINK ABOUT
Since America is typically represented by an eagle, Osama Bin Laden and Saddam Hussein should have read up on their Muslim passages. The following verse is from the Koran (The Islamic Bible).

Koran verse 9:11
--For it is written that a son of Arabia would awaken a fearsome Eagle. The wrath of the Eagle would be felt throughout the lands of Allah; and lo, while some of the people trembled in despair, still more rejoiced; for the wrath of the Eagle cleansed the lands of Allah; and there was peace.
(Note the verse number)

I have seen this same statement on several church marquees, and I have often received it by e-mail. Every time I get an e-mail with this, the sender thinks he/she has found a treasure, when in reality he may have fallen for a lie. You will remember, I stated earlier that a Muslim can lie to his enemy, and it is even encouraged in their religion to do so.

I find that many Christians never check their sources, but if it sounds good to them, then they repeat it. In preparing this material I have made sure to document my findings and verify the information before stating it as authentic. It is impossible or at least very difficult to win at anything when using false information and especially so in a spiritual warfare. I believe many of these authors writing about Islam have presented truth in their writings, but it has been interwoven with false and misleading information. This type of information will cripple the reader and hinder him from being victorious. God wants us to go forth with the truth of His Word, His Wisdom, and His Way.

> *1 Corinthians 5:6 Your glorying is not good. Know ye not that a little leaven leaveneth the whole lump?*
>
> *Galatians 5:9 A little leaven leaveneth the whole lump.*
>
> *Proverbs 16:25 There is a way that seemeth right unto a man, but the end thereof are the ways of death.*
>
> *Proverbs 24:6 For by wise counsel thou shalt make thy war:*

One thing I have noticed as a common thread about every book on Islam that I have picked up is the fact that all of these books kept saying the Qur'an says or the Qur'an teaches. So, I got a Qur'an for myself and began to check it out. The Qur'an I have is the translation by Abdullah Yusuf Ali, which is one of the most accepted English translations available. This will be discussed in greater detail later in the text. I even have this translation on my computer so that I can do word searches and studies. As a matter of fact the majority of the information that is most useful and effective in winning a Muslim to Christ has come directly from their Qur'an and not the writings of others that have claimed to be saved out of Islam.

When I got the Qur'an and started checking out what these books were telling me, I found that much of what the other authors said the Qur'an says or was saying was simply not accurate. This raised questions in my mind. "Are they deliberately trying to be misleading to Christian readers?" "Are they targeting non-Christian readers that they are trying to influence?" You decide for yourself as we continue to look at the evidence presented in the materials I have compiled.

When I loaded the Qur'an on my computer so that I could do word searches, I found an amazing thing. I found that the word "eagle" from the Qur'an verse that was printed in the church bulletin was not even found one time in the entire Qur'an in the English translation.

What caused me to do the search for the word eagle was the fact that when I read the church bulletin, I liked what I read. Therefore, I wanted to verify it before I used it in my teachings.

The following is what the Qur'an actually contained when I looked up the Qur'an surah 9:11.

> *Qur'an surah 9:11 But even so, if they repent, establish regular prayers, and practice regular charity,-- they are your brethren in Faith: Thus do We explain the Signs in detail, for those who understand.*

7

Compared to what the church bulletin said.

> *Koran verse 9:11 --For it is written that a son of Arabia would awaken a fearsome Eagle. The wrath of the Eagle would be felt throughout the lands of Allah; and lo, while some of the people trembled in despair, still more rejoiced; for the wrath of the Eagle cleansed the lands of Allah; and there was peace.*

As you can see for yourself, it is not anything like what was printed in the church bulletin. I believe that information like this has been put forth by Muslims to mislead and make Christians look foolish in the eyes of the rest of the world.

There is a war going on spiritually, and we as God's children had better prepare for the battle. Information like this will have Christians going into battle with faulty equipment and destined for failure. This is not God's will for us; God wants us to be victorious in our lives and in the battles that we fight for Him.

> *Romans 8:37 Nay, in all these things we are more than conquerors through him that loved us.*
>
> *Romans 8:31 What shall we then say to these things? If God be for us, who can be against us?*
>
> *2 Timothy 2:15 Study to shew thyself approved unto God, a workman that needeth not to be ashamed, rightly dividing the word of truth.*
>
> *Psalms 119:130 The entrance of thy words giveth light; it giveth understanding unto the simple.*

My desire is to see God's people as prepared as they can possibly be to reach the Muslim with the Gospel of Jesus Christ. We have a mandate to carry out, and we need to get ready to do it. We must be properly prepared for the task. This mandate is the Gospel, and it is going to require preparation for the spiritual battle that lies ahead.

> *Matthew 28:19-20 Go ye therefore, and teach all nations, baptizing them in the name of the Father, and of the Son, and of the Holy Ghost:*
> *20 Teaching them to observe all things whatsoever I have commanded you: and, lo, I am with you alway, even unto the end of the world. Amen.*
>
> *Mark 16:15 And he said unto them, Go ye into all the world, and preach the gospel to every creature.*
>
> *Romans 10:13 For whosoever shall call upon the name of the Lord shall be saved.*
>
> *Romans 10:17 So then faith cometh by hearing, and hearing by the word of God.*
>
> *Luke 1:79 To give light to them that sit in darkness and in the shadow of death, to guide our feet into the way of peace.*
>
> *Matthew 5:16 Let your light so shine before men, that they may see your good works, and glorify your Father which is in heaven.*
>
> *John 20:21 Then said Jesus to them again, Peace be unto you: as my Father hath sent me, even so send I you.*

According to God's Word it is not a request but a command for us to go forth and let our lights shine before men, and it is not up to us to decide which men to let it shine before. Therefore, the Muslim is among those that God wants to see our light. If this is what God wants, then we had better conform to His wishes and not ours. God can reach them, and I believe that He wishes to use us to do so. However, most Christians never approach a Muslim because we have decided that they are not reachable. This is exactly what the devil wants us to think, and in doing so we will neglect a large segment of the population of the world that God so loved.

If God loved them enough to give His only begotten Son to die for them, how can I justify hating those that Jesus died for? We need to be willing to learn how to reach them, and it is going to take a great effort on our part to do so. How much is a soul worth to you?

CHAPTER I
THE STRATEGY
TO REACH THE MUSLIM

As I stated earlier, I started out with the purpose of getting Muslims out of the way when we entered the prisons. The main reason for this was that I, like most Christians, had developed a virtual hatred for them. I not only hated their sins, but because of their actions I had allowed the devil to put hatred in my heart towards the person too. We could all probably say that we certainly have valid reasons for this attitude in light of events that have taken place.

The Muslim in recent years had become a great nuisance to our revival teams as we entered the prisons to try to lead people to Christ. They had become very confrontational and a very great hindrance to sharing the Gospel with the prisoners. They would see us talking to someone and would interrupt and try to cause an argument or distract the person to whom we were talking.

They would attack our Bible and Christian beliefs, trying to show Christian beliefs to be inferior to their own Muslim beliefs. They would come with lists of Bible passages that to the natural man (lost man) would seem contradictory. They would not allow you time to answer their question concerning a Bible passage that they said was an error or a contradiction, until they were bringing up another verse trying to discredit it as well. They would not give you a chance to prove the validity of the Scriptures. This would frustrate you to the point that you wanted them to leave you alone. It could almost make you bitter towards them, and even cause you to hate them, for you would see them as an enemy of the Gospel of

Christ.

However, God reminded me that He had given His Son to die for them as much as He had given His Son to die for you and me. I am to hate the sin but not the sinner. We so easily forget this when we deal with those that are so against our beliefs and ways. God reminded me that we were once His enemies too. God's Word tells us that we are to pray for our enemies, and I had failed at this. God had now burdened my heart to reach them with His Word.

I knew that before you could reach anyone you first had to get their attention, and they have to be willing to listen, actually wanting to hear what you have to say. In order to do this you must find where their heart or interest is and begin there. For the Muslim the Bible is not where their heart is, for they have been so indoctrinated to believe that the Bible has been rewritten and rewritten until it is so corrupted that you can no longer trust what it has to say. Their faith is established upon the teachings of the Qur'an.

The Qur'an then is what seems to be standing in the way of their believing the truths of the Bible. Therefore, we have a task before us to remove the obstacles that stand in the way of the truth of God's Word. This is much like the task Nehemiah had of rebuilding the walls of the city that had been destroyed.

> *Nehemiah 4:10 And Judah said, The strength of the bearers of burdens is decayed, and there is much rubbish; so that we are not able to build the wall.*

Nehemiah saw that they could not build the wall until the rubbish was removed. The following verses indicate that he did not make a rushed decision but carefully surveyed the devastation and carefully planned a strategy.

Nehemiah 2:11-20 So I came to Jerusalem, and was there three days.

12 And I arose in the night, I and some few men with me; neither told I any man what my God had put in my heart to do at Jerusalem: neither was there any beast with me, save the beast that I rode upon.

13 And I went out by night by the gate of the valley, even before the dragon well, and to the dung port, and viewed the walls of Jerusalem, which were broken down, and the gates thereof were consumed with fire.

14 Then I went on to the gate of the fountain, and to the king's pool: but there was no place for the beast that was under me to pass.

15 Then went I up in the night by the brook, and viewed the wall, and turned back, and entered by the gate of the valley, and so returned.

16 And the rulers knew not whither I went, or what I did; neither had I as yet told it to the Jews, nor to the priests, nor to the nobles, nor to the rulers, nor to the rest that did the work.

17 Then said I unto them, Ye see the distress that we are in, how Jerusalem lieth waste, and the gates thereof are burned with fire: come, and let us build up the wall of Jerusalem, that we be no more a reproach.

18 Then I told them of the hand of my God which was good upon me; as also the king's words that he had spoken unto me. And they said, Let us rise up and build. So they strengthened their hands for this good work.

19 But when Sanballat the Horonite, and Tobiah the servant, the Ammonite, and Geshem the Arabian, heard it, they laughed us to scorn, and despised us,

and said, What is this thing that ye do? will ye rebel
against the king?
20 Then answered I them, and said unto them, The
God of heaven, he will prosper us; therefore we his
servants will arise and build: but ye have no
portion, nor right, nor memorial, in Jerusalem.

My goal had been to get the Muslim out of the way so that we could witness to those that wanted to hear. As I researched extensively their beliefs and practices, I could see how the god of this world had blinded their minds. I began to see that I was condemning the sinner along with the sin, and I was convicted that I had not prayed for them as I should have because I was not seeing them as God saw them.

Yes, they are enemies of Christians, but what has God commanded us Christians to do concerning our enemies? At what have Christians failed so miserably? We have failed at praying for our enemies! We have allowed the devil to sow hatred in our hearts toward those that do not agree with us. We have begun to hate the person as much as we do their actions. We are to hate the actions or the acts of sinners, but we must never stop loving the sinner. I believe that we are never more like Christ than when we love and pray for our enemies. Thank God He loved and prayed for us. Thank God He loved us enough to sacrifice for us that we might be saved. What an impact we could have if we would love and pray that way too.

Romans 5:10 For if, when we were enemies, we
were reconciled to God by the death of his Son,
much more, being reconciled, we shall be saved by
his life.

Matthew 5:44 But I say unto you, Love your
enemies, bless them that curse you, do good to them

14

that hate you, and pray for them which despitefully use you, and persecute you;

Luke 6:27 But I say unto you which hear, Love your enemies, do good to them which hate you,

Luke 6:35 But love ye your enemies, and do good, and lend, hoping for nothing again; and your reward shall be great, and ye shall be the children of the Highest: for he is kind unto the unthankful and to the evil.

We must remember from where God has brought us as well as to where He has brought us. We, ourselves, were once the enemies of God, yet God loved us and gave His Son as a sacrifice for our sins that He might save us. The Muslim is no more of an enemy to God than we were. Sometimes we forget that we were not always on God's side. Notice again what Romans 5:10 says concerning being an enemy.

Romans 5:10 For if, when we were enemies, we were reconciled to God by the death of his Son, much more, being reconciled, we shall be saved by his life.

Colossians 1:21 And you, that were sometime alienated and enemies in your mind by wicked works, yet now hath he reconciled

Ephesians 5:8 For ye were sometimes darkness, but now are ye light in the Lord: walk as children of light:

Well, may I say that God began to break my heart for them and to remind me that they have souls for whom He gave His only begotten Son as well.

> *John 3:16 For God so loved the world, that he gave*
> *his only begotten Son, that whosoever believeth in*
> *him should not perish, but have everlasting life.*

The focus of my study then totally changed, and the goal became finding a way to get them to listen to what the Bible has to say. However, the problem is that they do not believe the Bible. So I had to find a way to remove what was standing in the way of their believing the Bible. We learn from Nehemiah that we need to remove the rubbish that is in the way, so that we can begin to build with the Bible. God began to let me see that the problem I was faced with was much like the rebuilding of the walls of Jerusalem. They had to get rid of the rubbish before they could build, and so do we. This is the strategy that God had impressed upon me. Work on removing the rubbish first, and then we can begin to build.

The Qur'an was the obstruction and how we were going to remove it was the task before us. I have found from past experience that many times the strategy that Muslims use is very often the best strategy to counter them.

I do not recommend that a Christian study the Qur'an or the religion of Islam. I want to mention that I use the term Christian to include professors and possessors. In many cases the conversions to Islam include a large number of those that professed to be Christian but were not truly saved. Most professing Christians do not spend adequate time in the study of their Bible, and this is why it is so dangerous for them to study other religions.

When a person is not adequately grounded doctrinally in the Word of God, he will have many questions that he feels his religion or his understanding of the Bible does not answer. One

16

may then be swayed to other religions or beliefs as a result of a lack of knowledge or understanding of God's Word.

> *I Corinthians 2:14 But the natural man receiveth not the things of the Spirit of God: for they are foolishness unto him: neither can he know them, because they are spiritually discerned.*

Many are seeking to understand from the natural man's point of view, and you can be assured that the Qur'an and the Islamic religion will certainly appeal to the natural man much more than the Bible and Christianity will. The devil will make certain that it does.

I have accessed the internet and typed in the search engine "turning to Islam," and the majority of the converts giving their testimony as to why they turned to Islam is that Islam answered their questions so that they could understand. According to I Corinthians 2:14, we know that the natural man cannot understand the things of God apart from the Spirit of God who reveals them. We should know then that human logic or intellect will never explain God's ways, and this is the testimony of almost all of those that have turned from other religions to Islam. They say it makes sense.

I have found it true that most Muslims know more about Christian beliefs than Christians know about Muslim beliefs. This is why so many Muslims are influencing those that lay claim to Christian beliefs. They are unprepared to answer the questions put forth, and they seem to be shaken many times because of the seeming knowledge the Muslim has of the Christian's Biblical beliefs.

The Muslim is not prepared for someone who knows his own religious beliefs and Qur'an content to approach them in the same manner that they approach those of other beliefs and religions.

Please hear me out before you draw your conclusion on the following statement. I have found that the best approach to use to win the Muslim is to lay aside the Bible and deal with them from their Qur'an. Note the following:

First, you must remember that even though they say they believe the Bible, they really do not. They only believe the parts that they can twist to make fit their beliefs and to support the Qur'an.

Second, if they do not believe the Bible to be true, but believe that it is corrupted and has been rewritten, so that it is no longer valid, you really have no foundation to build upon. They have been so indoctrinated to believe this way, and you will not change them by using the Bible since they believe it is corrupted. They may let you talk, but they are not listening. I know the Word of God is quick and powerful, but ninety-nine percent of the time that you are talking, they are really not listening. You know what I am talking about, because we have all done this when someone tried to convince us of something about which we already had our minds made up. The Muslim is the same way; his mind is already made up.

Third, if you bring the Bible into the conversation in the early stages, Muslims will only begin to attack it and try to discredit it. They will do this by showing you the list of verses they believe contain contradictions. However, we know that the Bible is inerrant and infallible. We must remember this as we speak with them for they have confounded many with their arguments who profess faith in the Bible. Remember, you may not be able to answer or even understand what they are asking or showing you, but they are approaching the Bible from a natural man's understanding. Thus, they will be influencing you into the same thought pattern. This is also their way of controlling the conversation.

You must maintain control of the conversation and keep the Muslim on the defensive. They should never gain control of the conversation. It is the natural response of most Christians to think they must defend the Bible when it is attacked, but in reality it is the Bible that defends us. The Bible is our sword.

Fourth, we will bring the Bible into the conversation, but only when they are ready to really hear what it has to say. Please, understand that I am not saying the Word of God has lost its power, is not able, or cannot accomplish what is needed in the hearts of the hearers.

> *Hebrews 4:12 For the word of God is quick, and powerful, and sharper than any twoedged sword, piercing even to the dividing asunder of soul and spirit, and of the joints and marrow, and is a discerner of the thoughts and intents of the heart.*

However, the key word is hearers. Again, we have already established that just because you are speaking in their presence does not mean that they are listening. They will use selective hearing until you get on a subject where they agree with you. You must have their ear before they will listen to what you have to say in order to have an impact on them.

> *Revelation 2:7 He that hath an ear, let him hear what the Spirit saith unto the churches; ...*

God has to be the one that gets their ear; we cannot do it. This is where many fail by trying to do what God's Word says that only He can do.

19

John 6:44 No man can come to me, except the Father which hath sent me draw him: and I will raise him up at the last day.

Fifth, God will use us to get rid of the rubbish that we mentioned earlier, just like the Jews did when they went to rebuild the walls of Jerusalem. The rubbish the Jews had to contend with was physical material. It took a lot of physical labor to remove, but it was accomplished.

The rubbish that is in the way of getting to a foundation upon which we can build with the Muslim is their beliefs, practices, and their Qur'an. These things cannot be cleared away in our own strength; this is going to be a spiritual task for which God will have to equip us. These things must be cleared away before they will willingly hear the truth of God's Word.

I Corinthians 3:11 For other foundation can no man lay than that is laid, which is Jesus Christ.

Romans 10:17 So then faith cometh by hearing, and hearing by the word of God.

Romans 10:14 How then shall they call on him in whom they have not believed? and how shall they believe in him of whom they have not heard? and how shall they hear without a preacher?

Ephesians 6:12 For we wrestle not against flesh and blood, but against principalities, against powers, against the rulers of the darkness of this world, against spiritual wickedness in high places.

James 1:5 If any of you lack wisdom, let him ask of God, that giveth to all men liberally, and upbraideth not; and it shall be given him.

Sixth, insert Bible truths and principles every chance you get, for God will open the way and give opportunity to do so. Through the material that I have compiled, there will be ample avenues opened to Biblical principles using their own Qur'an in which they put all their trust.

> *II Corinthians 4:6 For God, who commanded the light to shine out of darkness, hath shined in our hearts, to give the light of the knowledge of the glory of God in the face of Jesus Christ.*

The rubbish of which we have been speaking is spiritual darkness created by the Qur'an, but God can certainly make light to shine out of it. The devil will mix truths of God's Word with his lies in an effort to make it more palatable.

Many Christians are amazed when I say that I use the Qur'an to deal with a Muslim. However, there are some glimmers of light even in it. Muslims do not see these glimmers of light in it the way that we will see them, so we will have to show these glimmers to them. When we do show them these glimmers of light, they cannot deny the Biblical truth that we are revealing, and I have seen many amazed that such truths were in their Qur'an. What causes the amazement is that they know that it is a Bible truth that you have just revealed to them that they deny, but it came from their Qur'an.

You must remember that they read their Qur'an the way that they have been indoctrinated to believe and read it.

Islam does not accept some of the Biblically-based truths on which we will elaborate that we have found in their Qur'an. As a matter of fact these Biblical truths are strongly denounced in their teachings. Regardless of their teachings, the truths are there, and there is nothing they can do about it. A few of the things that will be brought out later are: the Death, Burial, and Resurrection of Jesus, Jesus is the Son of God, the Bible is declared to be the Supreme Authority, and the Fall of Man. All these truths and many more are denied in the teachings of Islam, but these teachings are in their Qur'an.

> *Proverbs 22:6 Train up a child in the way he should go: and when he is old, he will not depart from it.*

They have been effectively indoctrinated into Islam. The reason they do not see these Bible truths is because they read the Qur'an as they have been taught to read it. They believe as they have been taught to believe, and they do not question their teachings. However, when these Bible truths are pointed out to them, many of them will for the first time see it as we see it. Thus, a Biblical truth has been planted in their hearts. A little rubbish has been removed with each truth that we are able to share with them.

I always state as I share these truths with them, "This is not what you have been taught, but it is in your Qur'an." Then I say, "I wonder how much more you have been taught that is wrong, concerning the Bible and Bible truths." As we proceed we are able to see more rubbish removed.

> *John 8:32 And ye shall know the truth, and the truth shall make you free.*
>
> *John 14:6 Jesus saith unto him, I am the way, the truth, and the life: no man cometh unto the Father, but by me.*
>
> *John 8:36 If the Son therefore shall make you free, ye shall be free indeed.*

The truths that we are able to share with them from God's Word will have great impact upon them. God the Holy Ghost will take these truths that we are able to share and use them to continue to work in their hearts for many days to come. We have God's Word that He will work on them, and we know that it is His will to do so. The truths we share are like a fishhook with a barb on it; when it sinks in, they cannot just shake it out. The Holy Spirit will take that truth and work on them; it will be as though there was a barb on it and it will stick with them and be brought back to their memory again and again.

> *Isaiah 55:11 So shall my word be that goeth forth out of my mouth: it shall not return unto me void, but it shall accomplish that which I please, and it shall prosper in the thing whereto I sent it.*

> *II Peter 3:9 The Lord is not slack concerning his promise, as some men count slackness; but is longsuffering to us-ward, not willing that any should perish, but that all should come to repentance.*

How would you respond to someone telling you that red is black and that black is red, if you had been taught the opposite of that all of your life? No matter how convincing the argument or information is, you would reject it. You have been indoctrinated into a system of beliefs, your way of beliefs. You would have been shown a source for your beliefs and convinced that it is the true source of knowledge and information and that all others are corrupted. This is why the Muslim will not hear the Bible and holds to the Qur'an as the true source for right and truth. The only way to combat that is to find and show them the faults and corruptness of their Qur'an. This is what we will accomplish through this material.

Chapter II
OUR KNOWLEDGE OF
THE RELIGION OF ISLAM

Earlier I mentioned that many Christians really know very little if anything about Islam, except for what has been in the news since September 11, 2001. There has been a great deception promoted about Islam through the media. They are not and never will be a peaceful people as a whole. There may be some that are not filled with hate toward all other religions, but the majority that are following the Qur'an are not tolerant of Christians or any other belief, and they do hate and despise us. Their Qur'an forbids tolerating any other religions and commands hatred towards any other religion. Therefore, they will have to go against their Qur'an and its teachings to be kind or loving toward us and other religions.

On August 11, 2004, I typed the word Islam in my "search engine" to see how much interest there was on the internet concerning this religion which was growing so rapidly, and I was amazed that there were 9,160,000 results. On March 4, 2010, I again typed "Islam" and found 296,000,000. I was overwhelmed at how much of an increase there was. In just over 5 ½ years it had grown by 286,840,000 results. This time span is approximately 2010 days, which would put the rate of growth at 142,706 results per day.

I could never imagine that growth rate continuing and did not check any more for about two months. Then curiosity got the best of me.

On May 11, 2010, I repeated my search and there were 328,005,914 inquiries about Islam on my internet search engine. This was so amazing that it had grown by 623,725 results per day over the previous two months. Just in case my math was wrong, I went online the next day, May 12, 2010, and it had increased to 330,008,903. It had increased by 2,002,989 results in just one day. This one-day increase drastically illustrates the growth in interest in Islam.

People are much more interested in Islam today than they were before September 11, 2001. However, the amazing thing to me is that the religion itself has also grown at an alarming rate since that time and not just the interest in the religion. Of course, the references to other religions have grown on the Internet over time too, but nowhere near the rate that Islam has grown.

There are even textbooks now in our public schools where Christianity and Judaism are only covered briefly, but Islam is covered more extensively. In these studies on Islam they are required to memorize passages from the Qur'an, recite Islamic prayers, and memorize the patriarchs of that religion and their creed. These practices would be protested if they were related to the Bible or Christianity, but not Islam. You can verify this by going on the internet and looking up the textbook *Across the Centuries* published by Houghton Mifflin. It is a social studies book and is used mainly in the fifth through eighth grade levels. You will find lesson plans, activities, and resources; you can also read excerpts from the book that compliment Islam. Compare the space given for other religions to that of Islam, and you will definitely see the book is promoting Islam. Another textbook that is on the high school level is published by Prentice Hall, *World Cultures: A Global Mosaic* which was published in 2001. Both of the textbooks mentioned here were published in early 2001 and placed in circulation in our public schools here in the United States after the attack of September 11, 2001.

Many Muslims are now involved and hold positions in our government. They are helping to open doors for these and many other things to take place in our schools and indoctrinating our nation through our children.

The media has tried to portray Muslims as a whole as loving, kind, tender hearted, compassionate people that are misunderstood, because of a few extremist that claim to be Muslims. For someone to display these characteristics of being loving, kind, tenderhearted, and compassionate is not a natural tendency of our human nature. A Christian knows that we do not really know how to love until God first loves us, and we then have the love of God in us.

> *I John 4:8 He that loveth not knoweth not God; for God is love.*

> *I John 4:16 And we have known and believed the love that God hath to us. God is love; and he that dwelleth in love dwelleth in God, and God in him.*

> *John 13:35 By this shall all men know that ye are my disciples, if ye have love one to another.*

Our God places a great emphasis on love. He expects those that follow Him to manifest in their outward actions the character that reflects Him. He even expects us to love our enemies.

> *Matthew 5:44 But I say unto you, Love your enemies, bless them that curse you, do good to them that hate you, and pray for them which despitefully use you, and persecute you;*

26

Luke 6:27 But I say unto you which hear, Love your enemies, do good to them which hate you,

Even though there are Muslims that proclaim that they are a loving, kind, and caring people, when they are interviewed by the media, you need to look at the countries where they were born or raised, and where their religion is the dominant religion. These traits are not what you will see demonstrated within their borders. The traits that are demonstrated are harshness and cruelty. Their religion is one of complete intolerance of other religions, and there is no freedom to worship as one pleases. The Qur'an strictly and vehemently forbids it.

When doing word studies in the Qur'an one of the words I chose to look at was *love*. I searched the Qur'an for the character of love to be evidenced in the God of the Qur'an. Love is a characteristic of the God of the Bible and is so prevalent in the Christian's Bible. This characteristic of God is what has drawn us to Him, and has transformed us, and our nation, into the most caring and loving nation in the world. It is what has made America great in the eyes of the world. America is a nation founded upon Godly principles and the Bible. Oh, it is changing as we distance ourselves from God and His ways, but the love of God has been demonstrated throughout our history.

When we look at the Muslim world, it is quite different from ours in its very nature. To see the difference and understand it you have to get to the foundational principle. Just as our nation was founded or based on the teachings of a book (The Bible) that we have accepted as authoritative, their nations are also founded or based upon the teachings of a book that is authoritative in their culture. Their authoritative book is the Qur'an. It has shaped their nations into what they are and how they treat one another, as well as how they treat those who do not accept their ways. There is a definite contrast between their world and ours. I do not know about you, but I choose our nation unequivocally to any nation on earth.

When searching the Qur'an for the word love, I was literally amazed at what I discovered. We saw earlier that the word love, as it is illustrated in our Bible, has so impacted our lives and nation. After comparing the Qur'an and the Bible's use of the word love, I now understand why they are not known for being a loving, kind tender hearted, compassionate people or culture. The word *love* only appears in the Qur'an thirty eight times, and there are only four verses in which the word love is used. These are in reference to the love of their God known as Allah. Notice the use of the word love in the following four verses from the Qur'an as it shows how their God Allah loves. Keep in mind that our Bible clearly shows us that we love and are able to love only because God loved us first.

Qur'an divisions or chapters are known as a Surah.

Surah 3:31 Say: If ye do love Allah, follow me: Allah will love you and forgive you your sins: For Allah is Oft-Forgiving, Most Merciful.

Surah 5:57 O ye who believe! If any from among you turn back from his Faith, soon will Allah produce a people whom He will love as they will love Him,-- Lowly with the Believers, Mighty against the Rejecters, Fighting in the Way of Allah, and never afraid of the reproaches of such as find fault. That is the Grace of Allah, which He will bestow on whom He pleaseth. And Allah encompasseth all, and He knoweth all things.

Surah 9:7 How can there be a league, before Allah and His Apostle, with the Pagans, except those with whom ye made a treaty near the Sacred Mosque? As long as these stand true to you, stand ye true to them: For Allah doth love the righteous.

Surah 19:96 On those who believe and work deeds of righteousness, will Allah Most Gracious bestow Love.

According to the only four verses with references in the entire Qur'an concerning their god's love for man, it is dependent every time upon their love for Allah first or their having to earn his love first.

I thank My God that He loved me first, He set the example because He took the first step; He provided the way that enables me to love Him in return.

John 3:16 For God so loved the world, that he gave his only begotten Son, that whosoever believeth in him should not perish, but have everlasting life.

1 John 4:19-21 We love him, because he first loved us.
20 If a man say, I love God, and hateth his brother, he is a liar: for he that loveth not his brother whom he hath seen, how can he love God whom he hath not seen?
21 And this commandment have we from him, That he who loveth God love his brother also.

1 John 4:8 He that loveth not knoweth not God; for God is love.

1 John 4:16 And we have known and believed the love that God hath to us. God is love; and he that dwelleth in love dwelleth in God, and God in him.

Romans 8:35-39 Who shall separate us from the love of Christ? shall tribulation, or distress, or persecution, or famine, or nakedness, or peril, or sword?

36 As it is written, For thy sake we are killed all the day long; we are accounted as sheep for the slaughter.

37 Nay, in all these things we are more than conquerors through him that loved us.

38 For I am persuaded, that neither death, nor life, nor angels, nor principalities, nor powers, nor things present, nor things to come,

39 Nor height, nor depth, nor any other creature, shall be able to separate us from the love of God, which is in Christ Jesus our Lord.

Chapter III
The History of Islam

The reason we need to look at the history of Islam is to give us an understanding of their basis for existence. The better we understand their past the more effective we can be when we deal with them to show them that Jesus is the Way. Examining their history will clearly reveal evidence, that it was founded by a man (Muhammad). We will see man's ways of reasoning, reacting, understanding, explaining, judging, loving, and forgiving. You could say man's emotions in general.

The Meaning of the Word Islam

Let us start with the meaning of the word Islam. The word *Islam* in its simplest term means submission. When Muslims explain the meaning of the word Islam, they are speaking expressly of the name of their religion. Muslims say that it speaks of the religion of those who have truly submitted to God. Specifically, they would have you believe that Muslims are the ones who believe in the one true God whom they teach has no partners or equals and that it is only true Muslims that have yielded to his will.

Islam is the belief system of the religion. Those that are adherents of this religion or that follow this belief or that have surrendered or submitted to this belief are called Muslims.

You will find that there is no general agreement among Muslims even concerning their title, due to the many divisions, branches, and beliefs that exist among them. They are recognized by various titles and even different spellings under the heading of

Islam, such as: Muslim, Moslem, Muslim Brotherhood, American Muslim Mission later called Black Muslims, Baha'i Faith, and many, many other names or divisions.

Muslim is just another spelling but has the same meaning as Moslem. The title of Moslem or Muslim means one who is a true believer, or one that resigns oneself (to God) or is an adherent of the religion of Islam.

According to Islamic literature the word Islam carries a little more defined meaning. It is not just submission to God but to God's will. However, the word Islam according to many Muslims means a little more. Islam means submission to the good will of God and obedience to his beneficial law.

Islam is a monotheistic religion in which the supreme deity is God (Allah), and the founder and chief prophet or apostle is Muhammad. Muslims or Moslems are what they are called collectively, and all the lands in which the Islamic religion predominates are known as Muslim nations, lands, or countries.

Additionally we need to look at who Islam sees or recognizes as the founder of the religion. Although at this point when we speak of a founder, we are talking about who they recognize as the one that was used in the organizing of the religion, as it is known today.

The Founder of the Religion of Islam
Many Muslims will state that their religion was founded at the time of creation. Based on the Qur'an saying their God commanded all things to come together, either willingly or unwillingly at the time of creation, the earth and sky obeyed. It is because of this they would have us believe this makes the world Islamic by its very submission to the will of Allah.

Almost all Muslims recognize Muhammad as the founder of Islam. He is also considered to be the final prophet chosen by God to warn his people. There are two spellings for their founder, Mohammed or Muhammad; both ways are acceptable to most Muslims.

Much more will be covered concerning Muhammad later in the section dealing with the prophets of Islam.

The Birthplace of the Religion of Islam

Historically, the birthplace of Islam as a recognized religion can be traced to what is now known as Mecca, Saudi Arabia. At least this is where the Qur'an had its start, and it is the basis for the religion. Prior to this the only book of recognized Scripture was the Bible.

However, Muhammad and his followers did not remain in Mecca very long because of opposition. He and his followers fled to Medina and arrived there September 22, A.D. 622. It was not until January of A.D. 630. that Muhammad and his followers were able to return to Mecca, which was and still is considered their most Holy City. During the nearly eight year period Muhammad was in Medina, he gathered followers that helped him conduct raids on trading caravans from the city of Mecca. When Muhammad did return to Mecca, it was not because he was welcomed back but because he had gathered an army of more than 10,000 and laid siege against the city and conquered it. In the two years that followed Muhammad's conquest of Mecca, all of Arabia was united under this new religion of Islam. Mecca is still considered the most Holy City of all, where their most sacred shrine, the Kaaba, still stands today at the center of the great mosque. It is the focal point of Muslims all around the world as they conduct their prayers throughout the day.

Many Muslims will strongly argue that Islam dates back to

Abraham or possibly even Adam. Most will acknowledge that it was at Mecca that a more recorded recognition of Islam was established, as Muhammad received his first and last revelations of the Qur'an there. Muslims as a whole believe that Islam is merely a restoration of the original religion of Abraham, since they believe that he was a Muslim himself. They stress that Islam is a timeless religion because of its eternal truths. They believe it is the religion for everyone, and that it even existed before all other religions since it was even present during creation. This belief is based on the Qur'an which says that God spoke to the earth and the sky and said to them, "Come ye together willingly or unwillingly," and they said, "We do come together in willing obedience," which is Islam.

When Islam Began as a Religion

People that do not follow Islam will see Islam as beginning when Muhammad received his first revelation and began his teachings. The year A.D. 610 is when Muhammad received the first of his (114) revelations from whom he later recognized as being the angel Gabriel. There are no records outside of the Qur'an and the Hadith that indicate that Islam existed before Muhammad's first revelation.

Each of these revelations was later called a "surah" when they were compiled into the Qur'an. A surah is the equivalent of what would be called a chapter in the Bible. The first message that he received proclaimed that there was but one God and not many gods as the people of that region believed. The region in which Muhammad lived was involved in idol worship, and not just a few, but many, many different gods that were represented by these idols. So according to Islamic history, the beginning of Islam was during a time of much confusion, and no great spiritual leader was present to organize the people or give direction. It was a time when someone with leadership abilities could easily gain followers if he had the skills to do so, or could convince others that he had

34

indeed heard from God.

The Islamic community will not admit to this being the birth of Islam. Their claim is that Islam dates all the way back to Adam or Creation. However, there is no record of Islamic beliefs prior to Muhammad's revelations in the cave outside of Mecca.

As I stated earlier, many Muslims view Islam as a restoration of the original religion of Abraham after he had turned from idols. Some also believe that it dates back to the time of Creation and to Adam, based on statements in the Qur'an. To me there seems to be contradictory thoughts or even confusion about the point in time when Islam actually began.

It has been said that when Muhammad received his first revelation that great fear overtook him. As a result he spent days in the cave, and when he did return home, he shared with his wife what had taken place. Then he made the statement, "That which I have feared the most has happened I am demon possessed." It is also said that his wife, who was from a wealthy and influential family, convinced him that it was an angel of God that had spoken to him and had chosen him to be his apostle.

Of course demon influence would be denied by anyone in Islam because it would totally discredit their written authority in which they have put their trust for centuries. However, if Muhammad was convinced that it was an angel of the Lord that had spoken to him, I would think that he would have wanted to go back to the cave to get more instruction from this angel.

It is interesting to note that historically he received no further revelations for three years. Based upon what I have read from former Muslim authors, he was afraid to go back to the cave for fear of being possessed. There is no record of his going back to the cave for three years. I believe that as we proceed through this look at the Qur'an and practices of those that follow it, we will find that there is too much confusion in it for it to be of God. We know that the god of this world, the devil, causes confusion.

It is strange to note that only the revelations that are received in this cave contain mentions of an angelic creature referred to as Jinn. A Jinn in Islam is an angelic creature much like what the Bible refers to as devils, which can possess and control a person. This may be because of their presence in the cave and their possession or impression upon Muhammad when he was in the cave. Again, Muslims are not receptive to these implications or the influence of a Jinn in the life of Muhammad, but they do recognize them as creatures that do exist and that do have the power to possess people.

Islam's use of the Word Allah
As we examine Islam's use of the word Allah, it is easy to see this as the name for the Islamic God. The word Allah is even the title used for God by many Arab Christians. They are more cautious and descriptive in their titles now than they were. When the Arab Christians use the word Allah, they are referring to God the Creator of all, just as the Muslims do, but with very different understandings of who God is. Even in pre-Islamic times pagan Arabs used Al-ilah (Allah) the term used for the supreme God, which depicted or showed Deity. The word *ilah* was used when speaking of many gods.

Muhammad's own father had the name Abd-Allah, which meant slave of God. This was even before the birth of Islam, so the name Allah is not Islam's name for God but the Arabic people's name for God. There is no doubt that Christianity had made its way into the regions of Arabia, or what is now known as Saudi Arabia, as early as in the first century. Even the Apostle Paul wrote of going to Arabia. When Muhammad's grandfather named his son (Muhammad's father) Abd-Allah, he did it for a reason just as people in Bible times chose names according to events and things present at the time and as a remembrance. Therefore the name Allah was one that even the Arabic people had become familiar with, and they knew to whom it referred.

There is no doubt Christians and Jews lived in this region when Muhammad came on the scene, and he chose the name for the God of this new religion. He had been exposed to the teachings of both Judaism and Christianity in his early life. We do not know to what degree or to what level of understanding he had attained, but based upon his own father's name he knew something of Judaism and Christianity.

As we look at the Qur'an later in this material, we will see that it is evident that he did not have an understanding of the Bible. He was trying to express his understanding of God's Word from a natural man's point of view, and this is what was recorded later as the Qur'an.

> *I Corinthians 2:14 But the natural man receiveth not the things of the Spirit of God: for they are foolishness unto him: neither can he know them, because they are spiritually discerned.*

There is a possibility that Muhammad's grandfather and even his father may have been Christians. We can only speculate on this, for there is no evidence to support it outside of the choice of names that Muhammad's grandfather chose for his son (Abd-Allah). Muhammad and his followers on the other hand reflect no Christian character. Toward the end of his life, Muhammad did not even have a tolerance for Christians, even though he did in his early life.

Original Purpose of Islam
The original purpose of Islam was to bring the Arabic

speaking people to the knowledge of the one true God. Idol worship and polytheism was a very prevalent problem when Islam came into existence in the early seventh century.

Muhammad saw the need to try to bring about a unity among his people that were so divided spiritually. Muhammad was very much concerned about the many social problems that were present in and around the city of Mecca. As a result it is said that he spent many nights in a cave outside of Mecca that overlooked the city and pondered the problems of his people.

Today it is clear that this original purpose seems to have been laid aside. The purpose in our present day is much more of a conquering move with the intent of destroying all that oppose their views. Their objective is to use any means to overcome all opposition to Islam even to the extent of using suicide bombers.

A term very familiar to Islam is jihad (jih-hahd'), which is widely understood to mean "holy war." Many Muslims deny their belief in jihad, but their Qur'an teaches it. As a result jihad is what we are witnessing within Islam today. Muslims as a whole have become much more confrontational than they were in years past. Islam's reputation and religious history demonstrate that they have waged many wars in the name of Islam. Now, even though they deny this fact concerning their belief in jihad, we are seeing their aggressiveness and intolerance for other religions rapidly increasing in our present day.

Of all the different beliefs that we face in the prisons the followers of Islam are by far the most aggressive and confrontational of them all. They are also gaining a very large following in the prisons and in our nation as a whole.

The Final Authority of Islam
According to Islam the Holy Qur'an (Koran) is the supreme

authority, and the hadith is an additional guide to accompany it. Most Muslims will state that they also believe the Bible, but only parts of it, and then only if it agrees with the Qur'an. The hadith is their second most authoritative book and is accepted above the Bible in almost all instances.

An interesting note concerning the Qur'an is that it was not recorded at the time Muhammad received the revelations. He told his revelations to his followers who then memorized them along with Muhammad. Some were recorded but only a small portion of them, but the rest were only recalled from memory.

After Muhammad's death, many of those that knew the revelations by memory were dying in battles that followed. This caused a great fear among the other followers of Islam that the revelations would be lost and that there would be no true surviving record of the revelations. Even at this time in Islam's history there were already beginning to be variations in the revelations, because of them being memorized and not being written down. So a compilation was made in accordance with the order of the Caliph Othman or Uthman (spelled and pronounced both ways) twelve to twenty four years after the death of Muhammad. The compilation was then taken from any source that could be found, thus, bringing forth the Qur'an as Islam has it today.

The hadith contains the records and the deeds and sayings of Muhammad. This compilation was not put together until several more years after the Qur'an. People that did not even know Muhammad personally compiled the hadith, but rather these people knew people that had known him or had known people that knew people that knew Muhammad. This method of gathering the revelations was not the most accurate way of compiling a book upon which to establish your whole life and eternity.

The followers of Muhammad believed that God inspired

everything he said and did. These so-called inspired deeds and sayings were spread by word of mouth from family to family. Then in later years after the death of Muhammad, they were collected from those that had been present and those that had only heard of the deeds themselves, and written as an additional guide for the believers of Islam. The hadith is not one book that is consistent, but there are several variations of that book that supposedly contain the sayings and deeds of Muhammad.

The hadith was not to take the place of the Qur'an, but it was to be an additional guide for the people of Islam with the Qur'an standing as the number one source of guidance.

The Caliphate of Islam

The Caliphate was the ruling power in Islam from 632 until 1924. The word *Caliphate* means the rank, reign, or dominion of a Caliph. The word *Caliph* means deputy, successor, or supreme ruler.

This position originated because of the sudden death of Muhammad in the year 632. Muhammad's father-in-law and longtime companion was chosen as his successor soon after Muhammad's death and was given the title of Caliph. He was then in the true sense of the word Caliph (deputy, successor, or the supreme ruler) of Islam.

According to historical information that is available, it seems this new leadership of the Caliph believed that they had a mission. Their mission was nothing less than to conquer the world for Islam. Under the rule of the Caliph, in a period of about one hundred years, Islam had conquered an empire reaching from India to Spain. Their mission to conquer the world for Islam was rapidly under way.

Up until the Caliphate rule was transferred to a Turkish Caliph in Istanbul in the year 1517, the Caliph for the Shi'ites, had been someone from the tribe of Quraysh, to which Muhammad belonged. (*The division or branch known as Shi'ites came about in the first major split in the religion that occurred when Muhammad died. They believed his successor should be of his bloodline*)

The first four Caliphs for all of Islam were of the same tribe as Muhammad and were known as the Patriarchal Caliphate (632 - 661). The Patriarchal Caliphate covered a span of about 29 – 30 years.

With the murder of the fourth Caliph Ali, Muhammad's cousin and son-in-law, came a major split in the Islamic religion. The split resulted in the two divisions known as the Sunnites and the Shiites. Also, the Caliphate for the Sunnites (this group makes up 80% of Islam today) was then seized or controlled by another tribe or clan called the Umayyad clan.

It was Mu'awiyah of the Umayyad clan that stirred up much opposition against the family of Muhammad after the murder of Ali. It was he that said the Caliph should be a reward of piety and not just passed on by birth. Thus a major battle for control ensued.

It was a member of the Umayyad clan that murdered Ali. It was at this time that the major divisions started to take place.

The Shi'ites are not the majority by any means, but they are the more vocal and volatile of all the sects of Islam. It is the Shi'ites that took over the Iranian government in 1979 and currently comprise approximately 90% of Iran's population.

The Shi'ites are the branch that believes the Caliph must be a direct descendant of Muhammad. The descendants of Muhammad however, come through his daughter Fatima. This is because Muhammad had no sons that survived their childhood.

Muhammad only had daughters that reached adulthood. Fatima was Muhammad's eldest daughter and she married Ali. Fatima's husband Ali is the same Ali that is Muhammad's cousin, which was the fourth Caliph.

The following Caliphates are of the Sunnah or Sunnite Muslims, which are the majority. They believed the position should be filled by appointment not heredity.

The Umayyad Caliphate (A.D. 661- A.D. 750) spanned nearly one hundred years with only two families that held the position of Caliph during this period. This Caliphate moved the capital to Damascus, Syria. With this move the Syrian army also became their base of military support. The support of the Syrian army allowed them to control the Arab areas as well as allowing them to expand their empire to other regions beyond.

The Abbasid Caliphate (A.D. 750-A.D. 1258) base of support came from the eastern provinces, and the capital was then moved to Baghdad, Iraq. Thus, the focus became more toward Iraq, Persia, India, and Central Asia.

Even though the Turks were converted to Islam, they played a major role in the future of the Caliphs. Up until about A.D. 861 the Caliph not only had control of the religious movements, but it even controlled the political movements. However, they are now limited to religious authority only.

In the 11th century the crusaders came from Western Europe to recapture the holy lands from the Muslims. These attempts failed to free the holy land from the Muslims. Then in 1517 the Ottoman Turks took control and moved the Caliphate to Istanbul, Turkey, where it existed until the 20th century.

During the history of Islam, it has been quite evident that there has been constant turmoil. This turmoil has been reflected in the fact that leader after leader has been murdered by his own people. This has even continued into modern day with the example of Malcom-X being murdered by some of his own followers.

For a religion that boasts the claim that they are so united by the same beliefs and goals governed by a book (The Qur'an) that has never been changed, there seems to have been a great deal of disagreement. The many different branches or divisions that exist today verify this. Also, they boast that the Qur'an has never been altered, while at the same time saying the Bible has been rewritten over and over again. The Bible being altered and corrupted is the major argument that they give for why the Qur'an came into existence. This will be covered in more detail later in the book.

The Prayers of Islam

There are two types of prayers according to Islamic beliefs. The first is on a personal level. This prayer is to be personal, spontaneous, and devotional. It is not limited by boundaries of rituals or formulas.

The other type of prayer is ritual. This type is most often a congregational type. This prayer is composed of specific words and postures and is offered five times each day. The prayer times are at sunrise, midday, mid-afternoon, sunset, and before going to bed. These prayers are made up of several units in which the position or posture is changed. Some of the positions or postures include standing, kneeling, or lying prostrate. At the change of each posture or position the person must recite the words "God is great."

Muslims even use prayer beads though it is not clear exactly when Muslims adopted the use of prayer beads. These prayer beads are known as subha ("to exalt"). Muslim prayer beads usually exist in sets of ninety-nine counting beads and an elongated terminal bead. The counting beads are used to recite the ninety-nine attributes of God, while the terminal bead is reserved for reciting the name of Allah. Though the number of beads is important, the type of beads used does not represent the importance it does in Hinduism and Buddhism

Islam does elevate Friday above the other days to a degree. Friday is their main day of communal worship known as jumah prayer. This is the prayer time at noon or midday. It almost always includes other elements with their prayer time. Reading from the Qur'an and many times a message delivered by the imam will be included in jumah prayer time.

The Fasting of Islam

The word Ramadan means the hot month and is also the ninth month of the Muslim calendar. It is a period of fasting from sunrise to sunset. During the daylight hours all eating and drinking are forbidden. Those that are ill or those that are traveling have the option of postponing their fast until a later time for a similar number of days. This is not clearly permitted by the Qur'an but has been adopted into their teaching.

The month of Ramadan is set aside as Islam's month of fasting because this is the month in which Muhammad received or had the first Qur'an surah revealed to him. This month is therefore considered a holy time.

The Kaaba of Islam

According to the *World Book Encyclopedia*.

KAABA, KAH buh, also spelled CAABA, is the most sacred shrine of Islam. It is a small, cube-shaped building with a flat roof near the center of the Great Mosque in Mecca. Muslims everywhere turn their faces toward the Kaaba when they pray. The famous Black Stone, enclosed in a silver ring, rests in the eastern corner of the Kaaba. According to Muslim tradition, the Kaaba was originally built by Abraham and Ishmael, and the Black Stone was given to Abraham by the angel Gabriel. The Kaaba is the chief goal of the annual pilgrimage of Muslims. Pilgrims run and walk around it seven times, praying and reciting verses from the Qur'an. They touch or kiss the stone to end the ceremony.

According to the Qur'an.
The Ka'bah, was built by Abraham.

Surah 2:125-127 *Remember We made the House A place of assembly for men And a place of safety; And take ye the Station Of Abraham as a place Of prayer; and We covenanted With Abraham and Isma`il, That they should sanctify My House for those who Compass it round, or use it As a retreat, or bow, or Prostrate themselves (therein In Prayer). 126 And remember Abraham said: "My Lord, make this a City Of Peace, and feed its People With fruits --such of them As believe in Allah and the Last Day." He said: (Yea), and such as Reject Faith--for a while will I grant them their pleasure, But will soon drive them To the torment of Fire--An evil destination (indeed)!"*
127 And remember Abraham And Isma`il raised The foundations of the House (With this prayer): "Our Lord! Accept (this service) from us: For Thou art the All-Hearing, The All-Knowing.

There was to be no killing of game in the vicinity of the Kaaba.

> Surah 5: 94-96 *O ye who believe! Allah doth but make a trial of you In a little matter Of game well within reach Of your hands and your lances, That He may test Who feareth Him unseen; Any who transgress Thereafter, will have A grievous penalty. 95 O ye who believe! Kill not game While in the Sacred Precincts or in pilgrim garb. If any of you doth so Intentionally, the compensation Is an offering, brought To the Ka`bah, of a domestic animal Equivalent to the one he killed, As adjudged by two just men Among you; or by way Of atonement, the feeding Of the indigent; or its Equivalent in fasts; that he May taste of the penalty Of his deed. Allah Forgives what is past: For repetition Allah will Exact from him the penalty. For Allah is Exalted, And Lord of Retribution. 96 Lawful to you is the pursuit Of water-game and its use For food--for the benefit Of yourselves and those who Travel; but forbidden Is the pursuit of land-game-- As long as ye are In the Sacred Precincts Or in pilgrim garb. And fear Allah, to Whom Ye shall be gathered back.*

The Kaaba is an asylum of security for men.

> Surah 5: 97 *Allah made the Ka`bah, The Sacred House, an asylum Of security for men, as Also the Sacred Months, The animals for offerings, And the garlands that mark them: That ye may know That Allah hath knowledge Of what is in the heavens And on earth and that Allah Is well-acquainted with all things.*

The Sacred Black Stone of Islam

When it comes to the Black Stone, there are a lot of differing views. In the mid-1990s when I researched information concerning this, there was not a lot available. Basically, the famous Black Stone, enclosed in a silver ring, rests in the eastern corner of the Kaaba.

During the pilgrimage Muslims would kiss or touch the Black Stone as they passed around the Kaaba seven times reciting passages from the Qur'an.

Muslims believe that this stone was given to Muhammad by the angel Gabriel. Some say Gabriel gave it to Abraham.

Now there are over 6,160,000 web results for the Black Stone of Islam.

The following is from the "Wikipedia Encyclopedia" online:

> The Black Stone plays an important role in the central ritual of the Hajj, as the pilgrims must walk seven times around the Kaaba in a counter-clockwise direction. They attempt to kiss the Black Stone seven times, once for each circumambulation of the Kaaba, emulating the actions of Muhammad. In modern times, large crowds make it practically impossible for everyone to kiss the stone, so it is currently acceptable for pilgrims to simply point in the direction of the Stone on each of their circuits around the building. Some even say that the Stone is best considered simply as a marker, useful in keeping count of the ritual circumambulations (*tawaf*) that one has performed. Its black color is deemed to symbolize the essential spiritual virtue of detachment and poverty for God (*faqr*) and the

extinction of ego required to progress towards God (*qalb*).

The Black Stone, in Muslim belief, has its origin since the time of Adam. According to the Hadith, "it descended from Paradise whiter than milk, but the sins of the sons of Adam made it black." According to belief, an angel spoke to the great prophet Abraham, and told him to institute the rite of the stone in the pilgrimage at Mecca.

Muhammad is credited with setting the Black Stone in place in the wall of the Kaaba. A story found in Ibn Ishaq's *Sirah Rasul Allah* tells how the clans of Mecca renovated the Kaaba following a major fire, which had partly destroyed the structure. The Black Stone had been temporarily removed to facilitate the rebuilding work. The clans could not agree on which one of them should have the honor of setting the Black Stone back in its place. They decided to wait for the next man to come through the gate and ask him to make the decision. The next man that came through the gate happened to be the 35-year-old man and self-proclaimed prophet-to-be Muhammad. He asked the elders of the clans to bring him a cloth and put the Black Stone in its center. Each of the clan leaders held the corners of the cloth and carried the Black Stone to the right spot. Then Muhammad himself set the stone in place, satisfying the honor of all the clans.

The Black Stone consists of a number of fragments held together by a silver frame which is fastened by silver nails to the Stone. Some of the smaller fragments have been cemented together to form the seven or eight fragments visible today. The Stone's exposed face measures about 20 centimeters (7.9 in.) by 16 centimeters (6.3 in.). Its original size is unknown; its recorded dimensions have changed considerably over time as the stone has been repaired.

It is an irregular oval, about seven inches in diameter, with an undulating surface, composed of about a dozen smaller stones of different sizes and shapes, well joined together with a small quantity of cement, and polished; it looks as if the stone had been broken into as many pieces by a violent blow, and then pieced together.

> Visiting the Kaaba in 1853, Sir Richard Francis Burton noted that: "The color appeared to me black and metallic, and the center of the stone was sunk about two inches below the metallic circle. Round the sides was reddish brown cement, almost level with the metal, and sloping down to the middle of the stone. The band is now a massive arch of gold or silver gilt. I found the aperture in which the stone is one span and three fingers broad."

Ritter von Laurin, the Austrian consul-general in Egypt, was able to inspect a fragment of the Stone removed by Muhammad Ali in 1817 and reported that, "It had a pitch-black exterior and a silver-grey, fine-grained interior in which tiny cubes of a bottle-green material were embedded. There are reportedly a few white or yellow spots on the face of the stone, and it is officially described as being white with the exception of the face."

The Symbol of Islam
World Book Encyclopedia - the symbol of Islam is a Crescent and a Star, The symbol appears on the flags of several nations whose population has a Muslim majority, including Pakistan and Turkey.

Crescent, KREHS uhnt, is a symbol that resembles the moon in its first quarter. In heraldry, the crescent is usually shown with its horns (ends) pointing up. If the horns are shown pointing to the left of the wearer of a heraldic shield, the crescent is called decrescent. If the horns point right, it is called increscent. If they point down, it is a crescent reversed.

The people of Constantinople used the crescent as their symbol. When the Turks conquered the city, they adopted it as their symbol. It appears on the flag of Turkey. In Moslem countries, a flag with a red crescent on it means the same thing as a red cross on a flag in other countries.

The Growth of Islam

World Book Encyclopedia - Muhammad began preaching in Mecca about 610. He made slow progress at first. Most of the rich and powerful citizens scorned him and his preaching. His preaching angered and frightened the Meccans, and some of them even plotted to kill him. In 622, Muhammad fled to the city of Medina (then called Yathrib), where a group of people helped him. This emigration to Medina is called the Hegira. Muslims date their calendar from this year. In 630, Muhammad and his followers returned to Mecca and occupied the city. They destroyed all the idols in the heathen temple, the *Kaaba*, and turned the area around it into a mosque (Muslim house of worship). The Meccans then accepted Islam and acknowledged Muhammad as prophet. Mecca and Medina became the sacred cities of Islam.

The Spread of Islam throughout the Middle East and North Africa began with conquests launched from Mecca and Medina. After Muhammad died in A.D. 632, Abu Bakr was elected Caliph, the Muslim ruler (see CALIPH). He and his successors encouraged the jihad (holy war). Within a hundred years, Islam built an empire that stretched from northern Spain to India. The rapid spread of Islam engulfed the Persian Sassanid Empire and much of the Christian Byzantine Empire. The Muslims threatened Western Europe until Charles Martel defeated them at the Battle of Tours in A.D. 732.

Muslims united millions of different peoples into one great brotherhood. They established a splendid civilization in Iraq, Persia (now Iran), Palestine, North Africa, Spain, and Syria. They transmitted much of the classical knowledge of the ancient world, and built such magnificent structures as the Alhambra in Spain and the Taj Mahal in India.

There are no precise statistics on the current number of Muslims, but some estimates ranged as high as one billion in 1997.

I am sure that you have heard that Christianity is still the largest religion in the world, even though Islam is the fastest growing religion in the world. I have heard it said by preacher after preacher in pulpits across our nation, that the Christian population of the world is approximately 2.2 billion.

The statement that usually follows is, "so Christianity is still the largest religion in the world." I wonder if they are trying to comfort the people, alleviate their fears, or just what are they attempting to do. We need to be aware of the world situation, and not be like an ostrich sticking our heads in the sand hoping the danger will go away. We need to see the need to infiltrate these nations with the Gospel of the Lord Jesus Christ and start winning Muslims to Christ instead of hating them and seeing them only as an enemy. They are souls in need of a Savior.

However, notice that included in this number of 2.2 billion Christians, are Catholics, Mormons, Jehovah Witnesses, Church of

Christ, and all the denominations that acknowledge Christ as God.

The following chart of religions and their adherents is from the web site listed here:

http://www.religioustolerance.org/worldrel.htm

If you will notice, this web site has listed basically all world religions. The totals are listed in order of their memberships with Christianity at the top. This seems to be how everyone does it. However, their total for Christianity does, as I mentioned earlier, include many, many religions.

Vatican, May 1, 2006 (CWNews.com) - The world's Catholic population is now 1.098 billion, according to the latest figures from the Vatican's statistical bureau.

If you subtract just the Catholics from the Christian total which would leave you with 1.102 billion which still include all those other denominations and religions. I think you will conclude it is easy to see that Islam is the largest religion in the world today.

Religion	Date Founded	Sacred Texts	Membership	% of World
Christianity	30 CE	The Bible	2,039 million	32% (dropping)
Islam	622 CE	Qur'an & Hadith	1,570 million	22% (growing)
Hinduism	1500 BCE with truly ancient roots	Bhagavad-Gita, Upanishads, & Rig Veda	950 million	13% (stable)
No religion		None	775 million	12% (dropping)

Chinese folk religion	270 BCE	None	390 million	6%
Buddhism	523 BCE	The Tripitaka (consisting of the Vinaya, the Sutras, and the Abhidharma)	350 - 1,600 million (2)	6% (stable?)
Tribal Religions, Shamanism, Animism	Prehistory	Oral tradition	232 million	4%
Atheists	No date	None	150 million	2%
New religions.	Various	Various	103 million	2%
Sikhism	1500 CE	Guru Granth Sahib	23.8 million	<1%
Judaism		Torah, Tanach, & Talmud	14.5 million	<1%
Spiritism			12.6 million	<1%
Baha'i Faith	1863 CE	Alkitab Alaqdas	7.4 million	<1%
Confucianism	520 BCE	Lun Yu	6.3 million	<1%
Jainism	570 BCE	Siddhanta, Pakrit	4.3 million	<1%
Zoroastrianism	600 to 6000 BCE	Avesta	2.7 million	<1%
Shinto	500 CE	Kojiki, Nohon Shoki	2.7 million	<1%
Taoism	550 BCE	Tao-te-Ching	2.7 million	<1%
Other	Various	Various	1.1 million	<1%
Wicca	800 BCE, 1940 CE	None	0.5 million?	<1%

The following information is from the CIA.gov web site. The link to the site follows the information.

Religions and their percentages based on the CIA website:

Christians 33.32% (of which Roman Catholics 16.99%, Protestants 5.78%, Orthodox 3.53%, Anglicans 1.25%), Muslims 21.01%, Hindus 13.26%, Buddhists 5.84%, Sikhs 0.35%, Jews 0.23%, Baha'is 0.12%, other religions 11.78%, non-religious 11.77%, atheists 2.32% (2007 est.)

https://www.cia.gov/library/publications/the-world
factbook/docs/notesanddefs.html?countryName=World&countryC
ode=xx&regionCode=oc#2122

Now let us take a look at the growth rate of the world population in comparison to the growth rate of Islam over the last 14 to 15 years.

1997 - 6 billion, world population -- 1 billion Muslims
2012 - 7.1 billion, world population -- 1.8 – 2.0 billion Muslims

The growth of Islam has been at an unbelievable rate as you can see from the 1997 and the 2012 population figures. If you will notice the world population has increased by 1.1 billion from 1997 to 2012. Now, notice the growth of the religion of Islam, and you will readily see that the population increase of the world has been consumed by the growth of Islam. The religion of Islam has grown as fast as the entire world population has.

Islam's Basic Creed
There is no God besides Allah, and that Muhammad is the

prophet of Allah.

According to Islam's basic teaching, Muhammad was not just a prophet, but also the final prophet with Allah's final revelation.

The Imams of Islam

The Imam, or leader, is the chief officer in the mosque. The Imam's main duty is to lead the people in prayer. The prophet Muhammad led prayer in his mosque in Medina and in the mosque surrounding the Kaaba in Mecca. The Caliphs led the people in all religious and political matters, so they were the chief Imams. On special occasions, a distinguished visitor or religious teacher may lead the public prayers. Islam does not have an organized priesthood. Any virtuous and able Muslim can lead prayers in most mosques, but usually the Imam, chosen for piety or scholarship, handles the services of the mosque. Imam is used in the Qur'an to mean leader, guide, model, or sign.

Different groups use the title of Imam in the following ways in recognition of their spiritual leader:

1. Sunnites use the title Imam as a title for their Caliphs or leaders in their community.

2. Someone who is appointed by a local group to lead in Friday prayers.

3. Shiites claim only a person that is a direct descendant of Ali the son-in-law of Muhammad can hold the position.

4. Imam is also an honorary title given to a few of the most outstanding Muslim scholars past and present.

The Mosque in Islam

The mosque is a place of public worship in the Muslim

religion. It is where one prostrates one's self in front of Allah. All mosques, no matter where they are located in the world, must be built facing Mecca, and have in the wall toward Mecca, a niche to indicate the direction of Mecca.

Jihad in Islam

Jihad is commonly known to mean "holy war," but many followers of Islam say that it is the act of a Muslim spreading his or her religious beliefs, and correcting wrong, and supporting what is good. Many Muslims deny the use of jihad to spread their religion, but history proves that they have for centuries.

The Muezzin in Islam

A Muezzin is a crier who calls from the minaret of a mosque to summon Muslims to prayer. He does this five times each day during the times of ritual or group prayer.

The Mullah in Islam

Mullahs are those who are considered to be religious leaders or persons considered to be authorities in religious law. This is an honorary title and can be conferred on a basis of reputation alone, but most have received formal religious training.

The Minaret in Islam

A Minaret is a tower at the Mosque from which the Muezzin (crier) calls Muslims to prayer. This takes place five times each day during the times of ritual or group prayer.

Chapter IV
A Brief Look at Some of Islam's Basic Beliefs

Islam's Belief in One God

Islam's beliefs and teachings hold to the statement, "There is but one God, the creator and sustainer of the universe." This and many other statements on the surface do not seem to differ from that of Judaism or Christianity which are monotheistic religions too.

Islam believes that God is both compassionate and just. Compassionate because he calls his people to believe in him and to worship him. He is just because on the last day he will judge everyone according to his or her deeds. They also believe that on the last day the dead will be resurrected and will be rewarded with either heaven or hell depending on their deeds.

However, upon a closer examination of their beliefs concerning God, they are as different as night and day. These will be viewed much more closely in the chapter "The God (Allah) of Islam."

Islam's Belief Concerning Man

Islam teaches, "That man is the ultimate of God's creations, but that man is weak and frail, and that because of pride he does not see his own limitations but views himself as self-sufficient. However, because of man's own frailties, God has sent messengers or prophets to communicate God's will to mankind.

These messengers according to the teachings of Islam are all mortal men and receive their message either through an angel or by inspiration. They believe that man is prone to forget God and go astray. However, upon remembering God, man will repent and return to God. He will then gain forgiveness and will be restored to his sinless state in which he started life.

Islam's Belief Concerning God and Man's Relationship

The Qur'an teaches the absolute power of God as the creator of the whole universe. It also teaches that God is just and merciful and wishes for man to repent and purify himself while on earth so that he can attain Paradise after death. Therefore, God sends prophets with sacred books to teach man his duty to God and his duty to his fellow man.

Muslims believe Muhammad was the last of the prophets that God sent to carry out this task. They also claim that Jesus and the Old Testament prophets were the predecessors of Muhammad. Muslims believe that God has sent His messengers to all people at some time.

Islam's Belief Concerning Ethics and Morals

Muslims claim that the Qur'an sets the standard for ethics and morals in much the same way that the Christians claim the Bible does. Accordingly the Qur'an forbids lying, stealing, adultery, murder, and many other things. Punishment in the Qur'an is based on the Old Testament law of retaliation, "an eye for an eye and a tooth for a tooth." Unjust killing is punishable by death, unless it is accidental. If it is accidental, "blood money" is paid to the dead person's relatives. The Qur'an also permits slavery under certain conditions but urges that slaves be freed. The Qur'an permits a man to have as many as four wives under certain conditions and as many slave concubines as he desires. If a man has more than one wife, he is to provide for them equally, in material provisions.

Yet, in the religion of Islam divorce is permissible. They

believe that it is all right for the man to divorce the woman for any reason at all, but the woman has no right at all to divorce the man. For this reason many of the men will marry a very young girl and have many children by her and then divorce her when she is older and less attractive from the years of child bearing. The man then looks for another younger girl to marry.

This leaves the woman that is divorced with only one choice and that is to return home to her father, brothers, or uncles, until someone else desires to marry her. The chance of another marriage is unlikely because of the years of child bearing. It is for this reason that many women feel more affection for their blood relatives than they do their own husbands.

Permission for the number of wives is given in the Qur'an as is seen in the following reference:

> *Surah 4:3 If ye fear that ye shall not be able to deal justly with the orphans, marry women of your choice, two, or three, or four; but if ye fear that ye shall not be able to deal justly with them, then only one, or a captive that your right hands possess. That will be more suitable, to prevent you from doing injustice.*

The Muslim is given permission to marry up to four wives, but he is to be fair and deal justly with them. However, in the following Qur'an verse we find a contradiction to what we just read.

> *Surah 4:129 Ye are never able to be fair and just as between women, Even if it is your ardent desire: But turn not away (from a woman) altogether, So as to leave her (as it were) Hanging (in the air). If ye come to a friendly Understanding, and practice*

59

Self-restraint, Allah is Oft-Forgiving, Most Merciful.

The translator, Abdullah Yusuf Ali's Note 639 in the Qur'an states, "In this material world there are two principal causes of division between a man and wife, money and "the other woman" or "the other man." Money was dealt with in the last verse. Here is the case of "the other woman." Legally more than one wife (up to four) are permissible on the condition that the man can be perfectly fair and just to all. But this is a condition almost impossible to fulfill. If, in the hope that he might be able to fulfill it, a man puts himself in that impossible position, it is only right to insist that he should not discard one but at least fulfill all the outward duties that are incumbent on him to respect her."

> *Surah 4:34 Men are the protectors and maintainers of women, because Allah has given the one more (strength) than the other, and because they support them from their means. Therefore the righteous women are devoutly obedient, and guard in (the husband's) absence what Allah would have them guard. As to those women on whose part ye fear disloyalty and ill-conduct, admonish them (first), (Next), refuse to share their beds, (And last) beat them (lightly); but if they return to obedience, seek not against them Means (of annoyance): For Allah is Most High, great (above you all).*

Now we find according to the Qur'an that the man is even given permission to beat his wife if he thinks she has done wrong towards him or been disloyal. He does not need proof; he only needs to suspect that she has been disloyal.

Muslim men are permitted to marry anyone they choose with no regard for the religious background of the women they are marrying. However, Muslim women are not permitted to marry outside of the Muslim belief. Therefore, anyone that is to marry a Muslim girl must either be a Muslim or become a Muslim in order to marry a Muslim girl.

There have been many cases through the years of Muslim men marrying women even in America and having children by them. Then upon their return to the country of the husband's origin, they find they are not the only wife and are not permitted to leave. At least they cannot leave and take the child, for it must remain with him, and even their life is in danger if they try to leave.

I have an article printed off the internet from Fox News dated Friday, March 23, 2007, by Brit Hume. It is titled, "No Divorce Cited in the Koran." It says, "A female judge in Germany cited the Koran in her refusal to allow a Muslim woman permission to file for an immediate divorce over the abuse by her husband, saying that the Koran allows a man to beat his wife. The woman in question said her husband not only beat her but also threatened to kill her."

Islam's Belief Concerning Idols
The Qur'an forbids the representation of human and animal figures, so orthodox Islamic art rarely pictures living beings.

Islam's Belief Concerning Gambling
The Qur'an also denounces usury, games of chance.

Islam's Belief Concerning Consumption
The Qur'an forbids the eating of pork and drinking of alcohol. Even the consumption of anything containing pork by-products is strictly forbidden.

Islam's Belief Concerning the Blood of Animal Sacrifices
Islam's beliefs and teachings concerning "blood" resemble the

Old Testament sacrificial patterns in some ways. They do not see the blood as having any redemptive qualities though.

They believe that an animal is to be killed by cutting its jugular vein, which allows it to bleed to death, thus draining the blood from the body. They are to pronounce the name of God over the animal before cutting its throat.

Islam's Belief Concerning Virtue and Justice
The Muslim believes the Qur'an teaches honor for parents, kindness to slaves, protection for the orphaned and the widowed, and charity to the poor. It teaches the virtues of faith in God, patience, kindness, honesty, industry, honor, courage, and generosity. It condemns mistrust, impatience, and cruelty. Heads of families must treat all household members kindly and impartially. A wife has rights against her husband to protect her from abuse. However, as we saw in the case of the judge in Germany citing the Qur'an and from other Qur'an references that we looked at, the woman has no rights if the husband wants to beat her. It teaches that a person should not refuse requests for help even if they seem unnecessary. It is God who judges the dishonest petitioner and who rewards the giver in this life and the next world.

Islam's Belief Concerning Life and Death
Islam teaches that life on earth is a period of testing and preparation for the life to come. The angels in heaven record men's good and bad deeds and theses records will be used against them on the Day of Judgment. A person should therefore try his best to be good and help others, and then trust in God's justice and mercy for his reward. Death is the gate to eternal life. Muslims believe in a last day, or judgment day when everyone will receive the record of his deeds on earth. The record book is placed in the right hand of the good who then go to heaven. It is placed in the left hand of the wicked who then go to hell. The sorrows and tortures of hell resemble slightly those described in the Bible. To

the Muslim heaven is a garden with flowing streams, luscious fruits, richly covered couches, and beautiful maidens, but God seems to be left out of all of their descriptions of heaven. What makes heaven so great for us that are born again believers is not even alluded to by a Muslim. To a Muslim everything that makes heaven so great for them could have been had in their life while on earth. It is a sad faith that has no place of prominence or priority for God in their belief concerning their eternal home. Thank God, for us that are saved, it is Christ that makes heaven such a wonderful place to which we look forward. It is God that secures our great eternal home for us that are saved by the blood of Christ.

Islam's Belief Concerning Man's State
Muslims believe even though mankind is frail and not prone to follow God's will because of Satan leading them astray, that God is always ready to pardon and forgive. As a result of the pardon and forgiveness of God, He will restore the individual to the sinless state in which he started life.

Islam's Belief Concerning the Rights of Others
According to the Qur'an, Muslims cannot force anyone to be converted to Islam. However, they did in the early years carry out jihad (jih-hahd') or (holy wars) to conquer cities and countries so that they might impose political control over the societies and run them according to the principles of Islam.

Even today the Muslim nations do not separate religion and government. This means that as soon as they have a controlling voice, they will impose the Islamic beliefs on everyone of that country. Thus, there is no freedom to choose what religion or belief you want, but rather Islamic rule is enforced.

Islam's Belief Concerning Private Ceremonies
Private ceremonies in a Muslim's life occur at birth, circumcision, and weddings. The event that Muslims take most

pride in is a child's memorizing of the entire Qur'an. Devout Muslims that can afford to do so may even hire a special tutor to aid their child in the memorization of the Qur'an. At the accomplishment of this event the child's family holds a party for the student and the teacher, and both receive gifts.

There are also other ceremonies that are observed by all, which include the death of Muhammad's grandson, Husain, in A.D. 661 and the birth of Muhammad's daughter Fatima. (Fatima was also the wife of the fourth Caliph, Ali, who was murdered.) These are but a few of the important ones. There is also Ramadan and many others. The latter mentioned is observed by all, whereas the first two are honored namely by the Shi'ites. This is because Shi'ites are the descendants of Muhammad's tribe.

Islam's Belief Concerning their Mosque

The mosque, or Muslim place of worship, is the most important building for Muslims. The word *mosque* comes from the Arabic masjid, meaning a place of kneeling. It has a mihrab (niche) that points toward Mecca. There is a pulpit for the preacher (khatib) and a lectern for the Qur'an. A khatib (preacher) can speak, but it is the imam (leader) that starts the action of prayer. A mosque has at least one minaret (tower) from which the muezzin (myoo EZ in) (crier) chants the call to prayer. A court and water fountain provide for the ceremonial washing before prayer. The mosque is usually decorated with colorful abstracts and Qur'an verses.

Many mosques have a religious elementary school where young scholars learn to read and memorize the Qur'an. Some mosques, especially in Muslim countries, also have a madrasah (religious college) where students may complete their religious education. Madrasah graduates, sometimes called mullahs, may teach in a mosque school or a madrasah, or they may preach in a mosque.

The term masjid in the Qur'an refers either to the Kaaba in the Great Mosque in Mecca, which is the most Holy Sanctuary, or to other religious buildings in general.

In early Islam there were no required buildings for their common prayer to be carried out. This could be carried out anywhere providing the worshippers faced towards Mecca, Saudi Arabia.

Not long after Muhammad's death, his house was used as a model to fashion the proper kind of meeting place. This model place to pray, to meet at formally appointed times, as well as a place to hold political, social, and administrative functions that were related to Islam is what was later established as the mosque. The mosque would become their most holy place.

Chapter V
DIVISIONS OR BRANCHES OF ISLAM

Sunnah   (Known as the Sunnites)

Sunnah means well-trodden path. This is the largest branch of Islam. Those that belong to this group are called Sunnites or Sunnite Muslims. The Sunnites consider themselves to be the orthodox Islamists. This group embraces a much broader tolerance in contrasting trends in order to line up with Muhammad's statement concerning Islam's virtue of diversity. According to that statement no group would be excluded unless they directly renounced Allah or Muhammad. The Sunnites make up about 80% of the Muslim population.   This group believed that Muhammad's successor should be elected to the position of caliph.

Shi'ah (Known as the Shi'ites)

This group believed that the successor to Muhammad should be of the bloodline of Muhammad to hold the position of the caliph.

This group out of their respect for Ali, Muhammad's cousin and son-in-law, came to respect their community leader, the imam, as an infallible being. The imam was viewed as the only one that can truly know or reveal the true meaning of the Qur'an revelations.

There are only twelve imams that are recognized by orthodox Shiites. The last imam also named Muhammad will be the twelfth imam. They are awaiting his return to set up his reign. He disappeared in the 9th century and is expected to return near the end of time to inaugurate a reign of truth and justice.

Because the imam was the only one that could truly interpret the Qur'an, this narrowed the tolerance for different views. In the Sunnites the community's thought is what counts.

The Shi'ites make up about 10% of the world's Islamic population with the greatest concentration being in Iran. Shi'ah has for a long time been the national religion of Iran where 90% of the population is Shi'ite. It is from the Shi'ites that many other extremist, radical, and volatile groups have come.

President Mahmoud Ahmadinejad of Iran believes that Allah has picked him to prepare for the return of the 12th imam that went into hiding as a child in the ninth century. He and other Muslims believe that this imam's return will inaugurate the dominance and reign of Islam around the world and the extinction of the Jews from the earth.

Sufism
Just as in about all other religions, there arose an Islamic group that wanted more than rituals and outward observances. They were seeking after an inward experience. They believed that they must deprive themselves of all outward luxuries of the world, and devote themselves totally to pure obedience to God. These groups were very similar to monks. Their desire for communion with God compelled them to strive for a higher knowledge than what was granted to the average Muslim.

American Muslim Mission
(Better known as the Black Muslims or Nation of Islam)
This group emerged in the United States in the 20th century. It originated as an African-American religious and nationalist movement. In the beginning its theme was that all non-white racial groups should ban together to form one nation.

In 1913 Drew Ali, who was a member of the Nation of Islam,

founded a Moorish Science Temple in Newark, New Jersey. After his death its headquarters were moved to Detroit, Michigan. Wallace Fard Muhammad who was leading this movement was accepted by most of his followers as the incarnation of Allah. After his disappearance in 1934, Elijah Muhammad moved the organization to Chicago, Illinois.

Elijah Muhammad offered blacks a militant creed and encouraged blacks to give up Christianity, telling them it was only a tool of the whites used to oppress blacks. He encouraged their black members not to take part in affairs of the United States or to serve in the military.

During the 1960s the American Muslim Mission became known as the Black Muslim, but kept the title of Nation of Islam also. This group gained much prominence during this period under the leadership of Malcolm X.

In the 1970s Warith Deen adopted the name Nation of Islam. Then in the 1980s a man by the name of Louis Farrakhan became one of its most prominent leaders. He was an associate of the late Malcolm X.

In the 1960s a man named Cassius Clay held the heavy weight title in boxing. He refused to be drafted into the United States military, saying it was against his religion to fight. He then changed his name to Muhammad Ali and won his title again under that name. The reason that I mentioned this man was to show that he was following the teachings of Elijah Muhammad to decline taking part in the military affairs of the United States.

The strategy of Islam has always been the same. When the numbers are too small to take control, they lie silent. However, when they have sufficient numbers to make a difference, they rise up and get involved for one reason and one purpose: to control and to dominate with their religion and practices. They have begun to rise up in our nation and have already risen up in many nations around the world. They have already gained a controlling voice in many countries.

They have begun to show up in our military and in government offices on state and national levels. Their voice is now being heard in the United States, and Christians have been asleep too long. Many people are now fearful of what might happen or rather what is happening. I will say more on the matter later, but for now, I will say it has not taken God by surprise. God is just setting the stage for His return to call His church out of this world. Our home going is just around the corner.

Muslim Brotherhood
This group was founded in 1928 in Egypt. One thing that it does is strongly reject any influence from foreigners and especially those from the West. They follow a very strict observance of the Qur'an and the Hadith as their guidelines for all of society.

Baha'i Faith
There emerged a new religion known as the Baha'i Faith in the mid-19th century in Persia (Iran). Just prior to this there was a man named Mirza Ali Muhammad of Shiraz in 1844 that proclaimed himself to be the Bab (or the gate). He did gather a following, but he was executed in 1850 along with 20,000 of his followers. One of his followers that survived later proclaimed himself to be the prophet that the Bab had said would come. His name is Mirza Hoseyn Ali Nuri. This man is the founder of the present day Baha'i Faith.

They believe that God is absolutely unknowable except when revealed through appointed messengers. Among these are Abraham, Moses, Buddha, Zoroaster, Jesus, Muhammad, and most recently, Baha'u'llah. They believe that with each messenger we receive a greater knowledge because each messenger has come to reveal what is needed at that time.

According to their beliefs, one's purpose in life is to advance civilization and to worship God, the final goal being one religion. They believe that the practice of religion is for the purpose of bringing about family unity and eliminating extremes in wealth and poverty. This branch boasts of a prophet that supersedes Muhammad and has temples scattered around the world.

The following information is from their website on
BAHAISM:
Bahaism - religion founded in Iran in the mid-19th century by Mirza Hoseyn 'Ali Nuri, who is known as Baha` Ullah (Arabic: "Glory of God").

The cornerstone of Baha`i belief is the conviction that Baha` Ullah and his forerunner, who was known as the Bab, were manifestations of God, who in his essence is unknowable. The principal Baha`i tenets are the essential unity of all religions and the unity of humanity.

Baha`is believe that all the founders of the world's great religions have been manifestations of God and agents of a progressive divine plan for the education of the human race. Despite their apparent differences, the world's great religions, according to the Baha`is, teach an identical truth.

Baha` Ullah's peculiar function was to overcome the disunity of religions and establish a universal faith. Baha`is believe in the oneness of humanity and devote themselves to the abolition of racial groups, class, and religious prejudices. The great bulk of Baha`i teachings is concerned with social ethics; their doctrine has no priesthood and does not observe ritual forms in its worship.

The Baha'i religion originally grew out of the Babi faith, or sect, which was founded in 1844 by Mirza 'Ali Mohammad of Shiraz in Iran. He proclaimed a spiritual doctrine emphasizing the forthcoming appearance of a new prophet or messenger of God who would overturn old beliefs and customs and usher in a new era. Though new, Mirza's beliefs originated in Shi'ite Islam which believed in the forthcoming return of the 12th imam (successor of Muhammad) who would renew religion and guide the faithful.

Mirza 'Ali Mohammad first proclaimed his beliefs in 1844 and assumed the title of the Bab (Persian: "Gateway"). Soon the Bab's teachings spread throughout Iran, provoking strong opposition from both the Shi'ite Muslim clergy and the government. The Bab was arrested and, after several years of incarceration, was excecuted in 1850. Large-scale persecutions of his adherents, the Babis, followed and ultimately cost 20,000 people their lives.

One of the Bab's earliest disciples and strongest exponents was Mirza Hoseyn 'Ali Nuri, who had assumed the name of Baha' Ullah when he renounced his social standing and joined the Babis. Baha' Ullah was arrested in 1852 and jailed in Tehran where he became aware that he was the prophet and messenger of God whose coming had been predicted by the Bab. He was released in 1853 and exiled to Baghdad where his leadership revived the Babi community. In 1863, shortly before he was moved by the Ottoman government to Constantinople, Baha' Ullah declared to his fellow Babis that he was the messenger of God as foretold by the Bab. An overwhelming majority of Babis acknowledged his claim and thenceforth became known as Baha'is. Baha' Ullah was subsequently confined by the Ottomans in Adrianople (now Edirne, Tur.) and then in Acre in Palestine (now 'Akko, Israel).

Before Baha' Ullah died in 1892, he appointed his eldest son, 'Abd ol-Baha (1844-1921), to be the leader of the Baha'i community and the authorized interpreter of his teachings. 'Abd ol-

Baha actively administered the movement's affairs and spread the faith to North America, Europe, and other continents. He appointed his eldest grandson, Shoghi Effendi Rabbani (1897-1957), as his successor.

The Baha`i faith underwent a rapid expansion beginning in the 1960s, and by the late 20th century it had more than 150 national spiritual assemblies (national governing bodies) and about 20,000 local spiritual assemblies. After Islamic fundamentalists came to power in Iran in 1979, the 300,000 Baha`is there were persecuted by the government.

The writings and lectures of the Bab, Baha` Ullah, and 'Abd ol-Baha comprise the sacred literature of the Baha`i faith. Membership in the Baha`i community is open to all who profess faith in Baha` Ullah and accept his teachings. There are no initiation ceremonies, no sacraments, and no clergy. Every Baha`i, however, is under the spiritual obligation to:

- pray daily
- to fast 19 days a year, going without food or drink from sunrise to sunset
- to abstain totally from narcotics, alcohol, or any substances that affect the mind
- to practice monogamy
- to obtain the consent of parents to marriage
- to attend the Nineteen Day Feast on the first day of each month of the Baha`i calendar.

The Nineteen Day Feast, originally instituted by the Bab, brings together the Baha`is of a given locality for prayer, reading of scriptures, discussion of community activities, and enjoyment of one another's company. The feasts are designed to ensure universal participation in the affairs of the community and the cultivation of the spirit of brotherhood and fellowship.

Baha`i houses of worship exist in Wilmette, Illinois, United States; Frankfurt, Germany; Kampala, Uganda; Sydney, Australia; and Panama City, Panama. In the temples there is no preaching; services consist of recitation of the scriptures of all religions.

The Baha`is use a calendar established by the Bab and confirmed by Baha` Ullah, in which the year is divided into 19 months of 19 days each, with the addition of 4 intercalary days (5 in leap years). The year begins on the first day of spring, March 21, which is one of several holy days in the Baha`i calendar.

The Baha`i community is governed according to general principles proclaimed by Baha` Ullah and through institutions created by him that were elaborated and expanded by 'Abd ol-Baha. The government of the Baha`i community begins on the local level with the election of a local spiritual assembly. The electoral process excludes parties or factions, nominations, and campaigning for office.

The local spiritual assembly has jurisdiction over all local affairs of the Baha`i community. On the national scale, each year Baha`is elect delegates to a national convention that elects a national spiritual assembly with jurisdiction over Baha`i's throughout an entire country. All national spiritual assemblies of the world periodically constitute themselves at an international convention and elect a supreme governing body known as the Universal House of Justice. This body applies the laws promulgated by Baha` Ullah and legislates on matters not covered in the sacred texts. The seat of the Universal House of Justice is in Haifa, Israel, in the immediate vicinity of the shrines of the Bab and 'Abd ol-Baha, and near the Shrine of Baha` Ullah at Bahji near 'Akko. The members of the Hands of the Cause of God and the continental counselors are appointed by the Universal House of

Justice to propagate the Baha`i faith and protect the community.

Other Minor Sects
The Sikhism in India.
The Wahhabis in Saudi Arabia.
The Alawite in Syria.
The Druze in Lebanon, Syria
The Ahmadiyas in Pakistan. This is the most missionary active group in the west.

Islam now has an organized missionary movement with Al-Azhar University of Cairo being the intellectual center of Islam. They are presently working around the world.

Everything that God does the old devil tries to mimic or carbon copy it. God raised up the twelve tribes of Israel. So it is not surprising that the devil would also raise up twelve princes of Ishmael.

The twelve princes of Ishmael can be found in Genesis chapter 25.

> *Genesis 25:12-17 Now these are the generations of Ishmael, Abraham's son, whom Hagar the Egyptian, Sarah's handmaid, bare unto Abraham:*
> *13 And these are the names of the sons of Ishmael, by their names, according to their generations: the firstborn of Ishmael, Nebajoth; and Kedar, and Adbeel, and Mibsam,*
> *14 And Mishma, and Dumah, and Massa,*
> *15 Hadar, and Tema, Jetur, Naphish, and Kedemah:*
> *16 These are the sons of Ishmael, and these are their names, by their towns, and by their castles; twelve princes according to their nations.*

17 And these are the years of the life of Ishmael, an hundred and thirty and seven years: and he gave up the ghost and died; and was gathered unto his people.

Genesis 16:10-12 is foretelling about Ishmael and what he and his descendants would be like in the world.

Genesis16:10-12 And the angel of the LORD said unto her, I will multiply thy seed exceedingly, that it shall not be numbered for multitude.
11 And the angel of the LORD said unto her, Behold, thou art with child, and shalt bear a son, and shalt call his name Ishmael; because the LORD hath heard thy affliction.
12 And he will be a wild man; his hand will be against every man, and every man's hand against him; and he shall dwell in the presence of all his brethren.

Genesis 17:15-23 tells the account of Abraham making a plea to God for Ishmael that God would bless him and make him the promised seed to live before the Lord. God agreed to bless Ishmael but said that He would still bring forth the promised seed of Sarah just as His plan had always been. God would establish His everlasting covenant with Isaac as God had said. However, the world has reaped the consequences of Abraham's request ever since. I believe that God was not pleased with the request that Abraham had made based upon God's response in verse 22, when it says, *"And he left off talking with him, and God went up from Abraham."*

Genesis 17:15-23 And God said unto Abraham, As for Sarai thy wife, thou shalt not call her name Sarai, but Sarah shall her name be.

16 And I will bless her, and give thee a son also of her: yea, I will bless her, and she shall be a mother of nations; kings of people shall be of her.

17 Then Abraham fell upon his face, and laughed, and said in his heart, Shall a child be born unto him that is an hundred years old? and shall Sarah, that is ninety years old, bear?

18 And Abraham said unto God, O that Ishmael might live before thee!

19 And God said, Sarah thy wife shall bear thee a son indeed; and thou shalt call his name Isaac: and I will establish my covenant with him for an everlasting covenant, and with his seed after him.

20 And as for Ishmael, I have heard thee: Behold, I have blessed him, and will make him fruitful, and will multiply him exceedingly; twelve princes shall he beget, and I will make him a great nation.

21 But my covenant will I establish with Isaac, which Sarah shall bear unto thee at this set time in the next year.

22 And he left off talking with him, and God went up from Abraham.

23 And Abraham took Ishmael his son, and all that were born in his house, and all that were bought with his money, every male among the men of Abraham's house; and circumcised the flesh of their foreskin in the selfsame day, as God had said unto him.

Chapter VI
THE FIVE DOCTRINAL PILLARS OF ISLAM

When I was compiling this material in 1995 the things covered in this chapter were referred to as the Doctrinal Pillars of Islam. Today, Doctrinal Pillars, refers to a different list; and they are such things as prayer, fasting, and alms giving. In reality these things are not Doctrinal Pillars, they are practices, and I will deal with them as such later. This section is dealing with what would more accurately be called the Doctrinal Pillars.

The very definition of doctrine makes it pretty clear. The Latin: *doctrina* is a codification of beliefs or a body of teachings or instructions, taught principles or positions, as the body of teachings in a branch of knowledge or belief system. The Greek analogy is the etymology of catechism.

Often doctrine specifically connotes a corpus of religious dogma as it is promulgated by a church but not necessarily. Doctrine is also used to refer to a principle of law, in the common law traditions, established through a history of past decisions, such as the doctrine of self-defense, or the principle of fair use, or the more narrowly applicable first-sale doctrine. In some organizations doctrine is simply defined as "that which is taught," in other words the basis for institutional teaching of its personnel on internal ways of doing business.

Thus, the following five points are like the Muslim's constitution. These five things are the summation of their entire belief. We will look at each of these briefly now, but will spend much more time on them in the following sections. To be a true member of Islam one must hold to these five fundamental beliefs.

At a glance these five beliefs appear to be very similar to Christian beliefs. However, when examined in light of what Muslims believe about each of these we will see that they believe much differently than Christians.

Islam's Belief in the Prophets

Shahada – is the Arabic word that is used to express their profession of faith in God and the apostleship of Muhammad.

Islam's teachings concerning the prophet differ from that of Christianity in several ways. Even though there may be a few common views, they are still quite different overall.

According to the Qur'an, the prophet must be a human being. It is because of this that Islam teaching rejects incarnation or that Christ was God in the flesh.

Muslims acknowledge that God cannot be tempted. Therefore, God chose prophets to be examples for mankind to follow. They are again denying Christ as God in the flesh; because according to their view, how could God in the flesh (Christ) accurately serve as an example for mankind when we are so frail and have so many things that can tempt us?

Islam teaches that one qualification for a prophet was that he must be sinless or at least have never committed any major sins or faults.

So, according to their own teaching, the prophet has no room for error. At least they do not have any major faults or major errors.

We know that is not true according to the Word of God, for if a person sins in the least of things he is guilty of all.

> *James 2:10 For whosoever shall keep the whole law, and yet offend in one point, he is guilty of all.*

The prophet's message according to Islam consists of three parts:

1. The Unity or Oneness of God.
2. Submission to God's Laws.
3. Doing good works to attain Life hereafter.

Islam believes that if anyone was a prophet, these three parts would be the basis of his message. If this was not his message, he was not a prophet of God.

Islam also believes that in each particular community God has raised up individuals to warn His own people.

> *Surah 6:84-86 after recounting the story of Abraham, God declares: We gave him Isaac And Jacob: all (three) We guided: And before him, We guided Noah, And among his progeny, David, Solomon, Job, Joseph, Moses, and Aaron: Thus do We reward Those who do good:*
> *85 And Zakariya and Yabya, And Jesus and Elias: All in the ranks Of the Righteous:*
> *86 And Ismail and Elisha, And Jonah, and Lot: And to all We gave Favour above the nations:*

> *Surah 4:163-165 We have sent thee Inspiration, as we sent it To Noah and the Messengers After him: We sent Inspiration to Abraham, Ismail, Isaac, Jacob And the Tribes, to Jesus, Job, Jonah, Aaron,*

and Solomon, And to David We gave the Psalms.
164 Of some messengers We have Already told thee
the story; Of others we have not-- And to Moses
Allah spoke direct;
165 Messengers who gave good news As well as
warning, That mankind, after (the coming) Of the
messengers, should have No plea against Allah:
For Allah is exalted in Power, Wise.

Along with the names listed in the Qur'an 4:163-165, 6:84-86 the Qur'an also lists: Adam, Hud, Salih, Idris, Lugman, Dhul-qurnoin, Shuaib, Dhu'l-kifl, Uzair (Ezra), with Muhammad being the last prophet.

The five highest ranked prophets are:
1. Muhammad - the apostle of God.
2. Noah - the preacher of God.
3. Abraham - the friend of God.
4. Moses - the speaker of God.
5. Jesus - the word of God.

Some even include Adam - the chosen of God.

Based on the Qur'an alone, Abraham holds or occupies the highest position. Yet every time they list prophets, Muhammad is always at the top. As we will see later, their Qur'an has much more to say about Jesus than it does Muhammad, but they still esteem Muhammad greater than Jesus. Even common sense says something is wrong with their evaluation. I believe it is the devil that has blinded their eyes that they cannot or will not see the truth. They may remain blind to the truth until we can get the chance to show or reveal the truth to them from God's Word.

II Corinthians 4:4 In whom the god of this world
hath blinded the minds of them which believe not,

lest the light of the glorious gospel of Christ, who is the image of God, should shine unto them.

Islam's Belief in their Scriptures

Muslims must acknowledge their belief in the Qur'an as the true words of Allah as they were given to Muhammad by the angel Jibril (Gabriel).

The word Qur'an means recitation. The revelations were orally given to Muhammad (recited by Gabriel). This was also the means by which Muhammad was to pass the scriptures along to the Arabic-speaking people.

Muhammad did not write anything down, but gave the revelations he received orally to the people. Twelve to twenty-four years after his death it became necessary to gather the scattered chapters and pieces of his revelations and put them into a book for use in the Islamic community. This compilation of Muhammad's revelations is what is known as the Qur'an.

Belief in God (Allah)

In Islam's basic creed their belief in God is summed up pretty well. "There is no god but Allah and Muhammad is Allah's Apostle." This states their belief very plainly. Theirs is probably the shortest creed of any religion and is more than likely the most repeated of all religious creeds.

The summation of their belief in God would be explained by them as: "God is absolutely one and in sovereign control of all things, He has no equals or partners."

We will look at this in much more detail in the section "The God of Islam."

81

Belief in Angels

Islamic beliefs concerning angels are quite different from that of the Christian belief. There are some similarities but only a few.

They do recognize archangels as do Christians, but they add to the list. Christians recognize one by name, Michael. Islam recognizes four: Michael, Gabriel, Israfil, and Izra'il.

Gabriel or (Jabril as written in the Qur'an) is the messenger of revelation.

Michael or (Mika'il as written in the Qur'an) is the guardian of the Jews.

Israfil is the summoner to resurrection.

Izrail is the messenger of death.

Islam will acknowledge that the angels are created beings, to do the will of God. Another interesting belief of Islam concerning angels is the fact that angels cannot sin or disobey the commands of God. They must be obedient to God. However, we know, according to the Word of God, that in Satan's rebellion a third of the host of heaven rebelled and followed him. As a result that group of angels is reserved under chains of darkness unto the Day of Judgment.

Later we will look at three types of angelic beings as taught by Islam. The archangel, angel, and Jinn are the three types that will be examined in more detail in the section, "The Angels of Islam." Also we will try to see where Satan will fit in, which has caused some major controversy among Muslims.

Belief in The Last Day

Islam does believe in a "Judgment Day" in which every one will be judged according to his deeds. However, they do take a very different view from that of Christians. They do believe in a heaven and a hell. However the description of Islam's heaven and hell are much different from that revealed in the Bible.

We will look at both heaven and hell in more detail later in our study.

Chapter VII
RELIGIOUS PRACTICES OF ISLAM

As mentioned earlier, the information we will cover in this section concerns the current Doctrinal Pillars of Islam. You can see for yourself that these are not doctrinal at all, but they are practices of Islam.

To Recite
Shahadah - (To recite), which Islam says is to witness. Their belief concerning witnessing is quite different from the Christian. Islam's definition or requirements to witness is to recite their creed; "There is no god but Allah, and Muhammad is His messenger." They believe that to say this sincerely is all that is necessary to become a Muslim. To continue to repeat this creed to others and to oneself is their way of witnessing. At least it satisfies their conscience.

To Pray
Salat - the ritual prayer that is to be performed five times each day. In Muslim countries this would be the called times of prayer, when all are summoned to prayer. These times of prayer are: sunrise, midday, midafternoon, sunset, and bedtime.

Besides the five times they are summoned to prayer, they are to have their personal or individual prayer. This according to some sources is another twelve times daily. So, according to these sources that would be seventeen complete prayers each day.

On Friday at noon Muslims are required to gather at a

mosque for a time of prayer together. (Jumah) Friday, for Muslims resembles the Jewish Sabbaths, Catholic Fridays, and Christian Sundays. Muslims are expected to attend noon prayers at a mosque. There, a Muslim in ceremony washes his face, hands, and feet immediately before prayer. The prayer leader faces Mecca. The men stand in rows behind him, and the women stand behind the men. The prayers consist of reciting passages from the Qur'an and other phrases of praise to God. They include such movements as bowing from the hips and kneeling with the face to the ground. Friday prayers are preceded by a sermon.

To Fast
Sawm – (Fasting) particularly the Ramadan fast.

Ramadan was the month in which the first revelation or surah of the Qur'an was revealed to Muhammad. Therefore, this is the month set aside for their fast of Ramadan to commemorate the event.

During the fast of Ramadan participants are to refrain from eating or drinking during daylight hours for the entire month. As a matter of fact, the Qur'an forbids these things and many others during Ramadan.

However, during the dark hours they are allowed to eat certain things and in any quantity they desire. Many will eat and drink anything they want.

According to one source, the time when Ramadan is observed will vary because a lunar calendar is used. This is the Islamic calendar, and Ramadan would be the ninth month according to their calendar.

If someone is too ill or they are on a journey, they will be permitted to perform their fast at a later time for the same number of days. Also, soldiers in the field or on duty or nursing mothers are permitted to perform the fast at a later date.

This fast ends with a festival lasting three days. This festival is called Little Bairam. This is typically a feast of specially prepared foods, and they eat all they can.

To Give Alms
Islam's almsgiving consist of two types.

The first is an obligatory tax called the zakat. This has now become a voluntary charitable contribution in most Muslim states or communities. Some countries still enforce it as a mandatory tax. This tax or offering is 1/40 or 2.5 percent of their income. The main use of it goes to the poor and needy.

The second is called sadaqah. This is a freewill type of almsgiving to the Muslim community or Muslim state. This is usually by far the larger of the two types of almsgiving because it is used to further the cause of Islam. There are several verses in the Qur'an that strongly encourage this type of almsgiving if you want to go to heaven or be blessed of God.

To Make the Pilgrimage
Hajj – is the Arabic word for the pilgrimage to Mecca.

The Annual Pilgrimage or the Hajj to Mecca is commanded in the Qur'an. All able Muslims are required to make the pilgrimage at least once in their lifetime. Many ceremonies are required during the pilgrimage. The most important ceremonies include walking seven times around the Kaaba and kissing or touching the sacred Black Stone that is set in its wall. Because of the large numbers that now go to the Mosque during the pilgrimage, kissing or touching the stone is the preferred thing to do, but pointing at it as they walk around the Kaaba is acceptable. Most Muslims include a visit to the Mosque of Muhammad in Medina. The pilgrimage is concluded with the Festival of Sacrifice when the Muslims sacrifice a sheep, goat, or camel, and usually give the meat to the poor. This is the Muslims' Great Festival, while Little Bairam is the Lesser Festival. Muslims celebrate both of these festivals by visiting, wearing new clothes, and exchanging gifts.

The hajj (Pilgrimage) does require that all who make the pilgrimage wear a white garment called an ihram. By doing this it will eliminate all distinctions of class or social status during the hajj (Pilgrimage).

The hajj (Pilgrimage) is intended to reenact the hegira (Flight of Muhammad from Mecca to Medina in A.D. 622.) This hajj (Pilgrimage) usually takes a week or more, perhaps as long as a month. The reason for the long period of time is because there are several sacred sites that must be visited along the way.

If one is too poor to be able to afford the journey, they will be excused. Or if they are unable physically they are excused. It amazes me that many of the Muslims in America cannot afford to go to Mecca, but they can buy very nice clothes, cars, and jewelry. After making the pilgrimage, the person is entitled to be called a hajji to signify their accomplishment of making the journey.

The media has done much to indoctrinate our society to the things of Islam for many years. An example is a cartoon back in the early 1960s. The cartoon was Johnny Quest. In the cartoon Johnny had a little Indian boy as his sidekick. You guessed it; the boy's name was Hajji. It was implying that he had made the pilgrimage. I even saw an episode of the Little Rascals filmed in 1935 that had Islam characters being portrayed as good and upright.

Even in films of recent days, notice how many times you see a mosque in the background and many other things pertaining to Islam. We have been acclimated to the presence of the religion of Islam and its adherents to the point they have become common-place to us. We have gotten accustomed to their presence. Their Islamic attire does not stand out in the crowd as it once did.

Chapter VIII
PROPHETS OF ISLAM

Who Islam Holds as Their Prophets

Surah 6:84-86 after recounting the story of Abraham, God declares: We gave him Isaac And Jacob: all (three) We guided: And before him, We guided Noah, And among his progeny, David, Solomon, Job, Joseph, Moses, and Aaron: Thus do We reward Those who do good:
85 And Zakariya and Yabya, And Jesus and Elias: All in the ranks Of the Righteous:
86 And Ismail and Elisha, And Jonah, and Lot: And to all We gave Favour above the nations:

Here is the list of names extracted from the passage 6:84-86 of the Qur'an: Abraham, Isaac, Jacob, Noah, David, Solomon, Job, Joseph, Moses, Aaron, Zakariya, Yabya, John, Jesus, Elias, Ismail, Elisha, Jonas, and Lot.

Note all but two of these are men of God or Israelites from the Bible. The one (Ismail) is mentioned in the Bible but not as a man of God or an Israelite, and the other is (Yabya) who is not mentioned in the Bible by that name. However, in Islamic teaching and within their understanding, Yabya is accepted to be John the Baptist.

Surah 4:163-165 We have sent thee Inspiration, as we sent it To Noah and the Messengers After him:

89

We sent Inspiration to Abraham, Ismail, Isaac,
Jacob And the Tribes, to Jesus, Job, Jonah, Aaron,
and Solomon, And to David We gave the Psalms.
164 Of some messengers We have Already told thee
the story; Of others we have not-- And to Moses
Allah spoke direct;
165 Messengers who gave good news As well as
warning, That mankind, after (the coming) Of the
messengers, should have No plea against Allah:
For Allah is exalted in Power, Wise.

Here is another list from the passage 4:163-165 of the Qur'an: Noah, Abraham, Ismail, Isaac, Jacob and the Tribes, Jesus, Job, Jonah, Aaron, Solomon, David, and Moses. Again note that all but one are Israelite men from the Bible with whom we are familiar.

I have also listed several others that are recognized by Islam as prophets that are mentioned in the Qur'an: Adam, Hud, Salih, Idris, Luqman, Dhul-qarnian, Shu'aib, Dhul'Kifl, Uzair, and Muhammad.

I have included a brief explanation of each of these from the Wikipedia online encyclopedia, which gives a definition according to the Islamic school of thinking, with the exception of Muhammad whom we will cover later.

Hud is the name of a prophet of ancient Arabia, who is mentioned in the Qur'an. In the eleventh chapter of the Qur'an, Hud is named, though the narrative of Hud comprises only a small portion of the chapter.

Salih or Saleh (Arabic: meaning Righteous) was a prophet of ancient Arabia mentioned in the Qur'an, who according to the teachings of Islam prophesied to the tribe of the Thamud. He is mentioned nine times throughout the Qur'an, and his people are frequently referenced as a wicked community who, because of their sins, were ultimately destroyed. Saleh is sometimes equated with the Shelah of the Hebrew Bible; however, there is almost nothing in common between the Qur'anic narrative of Saleh and the Biblical narrative of Shelah. The preaching and prophecy of Saleh is linked to the famous Islamic story of the She-Camel, which was the gift God gave the people of the Thamud when they desired a miracle to confirm the truth of the message Saleh was preaching. Chronologically, scholars believe Saleh's prophesying to have been post-Antediluvian but pre-Abrahamic.

Idris (Arabic) is an Islamic prophet that is mentioned in the Qur'an and who, according to the Qur'an , was exalted by God to a high station in life. Idris is, at times by Muslims, identified with the Biblical Enoch. However, any true Biblical identity of Idris remains uncertain. According to hadith, narrated by Malik ibn Anas and found in Sahih Muslim, it is said that on Muhammad's Night Journey, he encountered Idris in the fourth heaven. The traditions that have developed around the figure of Idris have given him the scope of a prophet as well as a philosopher and mystic.

Luqman also known as Luqman the Wise, Luqmaan, Lukman, and Luqman al-Hakeem, (Arabic), was a wise man for whom Surat Luqman (Arabic), the thirty-first sura (chapter) of the Qur'an, was named. Luqman (1100 BC) is believed to be from Africa. There are many stories about Luqman in Arabic and Turkish literature and the primary historical sources are the Tafsir ibn Kathir and Stories of the Qur'an by Ibn Kathir. The Qur'an does not state whether or not Luqman was a prophet, but some people believe him to be a prophet and thus write Alayhis Salaam (A.S.) with his name.

Luqman was described as a perceptive man, always watching the animals and plants of his surroundings, and he tried to understand the world based on what he saw. One day, while he was sleeping under a tree, an angel came to him and said Allah wanted to bestow a gift upon Luqman either wisdom or prophecy. Luqman chose wisdom, and when he woke from his slumber, he was aware that his senses and his understanding had sharpened. He felt in complete harmony with nature and could understand the inner meaning of things, beyond their physical reality. Immediately he bowed down and thanked and praised Allah for this wonderful gift. Unfortunately, Luqman was captured by slavers and sold as a slave.

Dhul-Qarnayn (Arabic, ḏū al-qarnayn), literally "He of the Two Horns" or "He of the two centuries" is a figure mentioned in the Qur'an where he is described as a great and righteous ruler who built a long wall that keeps Gog and Magog from attacking the people whom he met on his journey to the east (i.e., the rising of the sun). According to a classical interpretation, the name is due to his having reached the two "Horns" of the Sun, east and west, where it rises and where it sets during his journey.

The identification of Dhul-Qarnayn in historical context is not clear, and therefore this subject has generated various theories. In modern scholarship the character is usually identified as Alexander the Great, who is ascribed similar adventures in the Alexander romance. The same opinion is held in traditional Islamic scholarship. In other modern scholarship the character is usually identified as Cyrus the Great. Some modern scholars also identify the character as Byzantine emperor Heraclius, who was celebrated by his contemporaries as a "second Alexander" and whose Persian campaign had inspired the Alexander romance.

Shu'aib, Shuayb, or Shoaib, (Arabic, meaning, who shows the right path), was an ancient Midianite prophet, who is mentioned in the Qur'an a total of eleven times. He is believed to have lived after Abraham, and Muslims believe that he was sent as a prophet to two communities, namely the Midianites and the People of the

Wood. To both people, Shoaib proclaimed the faith of Islam and warned the people to end their fraudulent ways. When they did not repent, God destroyed both of the communities. Shoaib is understood by Muslims to have been one of the few Arabian prophets mentioned by name in the Qur'an, the others being Saleh, Hud, Ishmael and Muhammad. It is said that he was known by early Muslims as "the eloquent preacher amongst the prophets," because he was, according to Islamic tradition, granted talent and eloquence in his language.

Dhul-Kifl, or Zul-Kifl, (Arabic meaning: The Twin) (1600?–1400? BCE), is an Islamic prophet who has been identified with various Hebrew Bible prophets, most commonly Ezekiel. It is believed that he lived for roughly seventy-five years and that he preached in what is modern day Iraq. Dhul-Kifl is believed to have been exalted by God to a high station in life and is chronicled in the Qur'an as a man of the "Company of the Good." Although not much is known of Dhul-Kifl from other historical sources, all the writings from classical commentators, such as Ibn Ishaq and Ibn Kathir, speak of Dhul-Kifl as a prophetic, saintly man who remained faithful in daily prayer and worship.

Uzair, Uzayr - identified with the Biblical Ezra (Arabic, 'Uzair, Turkish: 'Üzeyir) - is a figure mentioned in the Qur'an, in the verse 9:30, which claims that he was revered by the Jews as "the son of God."

Although not explicitly mentioned in Qur'an among the prophets, Ezra is considered as one of the prophets by some Muslim scholars based on Islamic traditions.

On the other hand, Muslim scholars such as Mutahhar al-Maqdisi and Djuwayni and notably Ibn Hazm and al-Samaw'al accused Ezra (or one of his disciples) of falsification of the Torah. Several sources state that the Qur'an refers to Jews who began to

93

call Ezra a "son of God" due to his religious achievements coupled with a misunderstanding of certain Jews with regards to his position in the Jewish faith as a Bene Elohim (Sons of God).

Note: Islamic teaching is trying to link all of these Islamic prophets with the Bible. Of course their argument is still that the Bible has been corrupted, but they can still use passages from it to try to validate their teachings. This is also an attempt to make their prophets a little more acceptable by others outside of their religion. So the use of a book that has been accepted by multitudes as authoritative will give more credence to their teachings. Islam, to validate their history, seeks the historicity of the Bible. However, I am sure that you have seen that it is a far stretch to do so.

The Qualifications to be a Prophet of Islam
According to the Qur'an a prophet must be a human being. This is one reason that they so strongly reject the doctrine of the incarnation (God in the Flesh) of Jesus Christ.

They must be men of good character and high honor. Their truthfulness, intelligence, and integrity must be beyond question.

They were infallible in that they did not commit sins or violate the Law of God. Most Muslim scholars believe that the prophets are completely sinless, or at least they have committed no major sins or have no major faults. As I mentioned earlier, if they committed what Muslims would deem a small sin or fault, it would be acceptable because it was not a major sin or fault. However, if they offend in the least of these, the Bible declares they are guilty of all.

Some scholars claim that even before becoming a prophet or receiving their first revelation, they were found naturally good. These types of men would shun any blameworthy actions or anything unclean. Islam teaches that they had an instinctive inclination to rise above things that were wrong in the sight of God. They seemed to flee such things as though there was an inborn hatred for wrong-doing. Again, we know according to the Bible that no man outside of the man Jesus Christ has ever been able to make such a claim of being sinless. As Christians we know that no man can claim to be sinless, because of who our spiritual father is when we are born into this world.

> *John 8:44 Ye are of your father the devil, and the lusts of your father ye will do. He was a murderer from the beginning, and abode not in the truth, because there is no truth in him. When he speaketh a lie, he speaketh of his own: for he is a liar, and the father of it.*

The message that the prophet proclaims is another qualification to be a prophet. If he does not proclaim the oneness of God, submission to God's Laws, and the need to do good deeds in light of the hereafter then he is not a true prophet of God.

Another qualification of a prophet is that he performs miracles. However, this brings up a very interesting point that we will look at in much more detail later.

The point here is that in the Qur'an there are no recorded miracles performed by or credited to Muhammad.

Islam's View of Sin Concerning the Prophet
There are different schools of thought on this subject. One is that the prophet was a person in whom the power of sin did not exist. Again, this is totally contrary to the Word of God.

> *Romans 3:10 As it is written, There is none righteous, no, not one:*

95

Romans 3:23 For all have sinned, and come short of the glory of God;

I John 1:8 If we say that we have no sin, we deceive ourselves, and the truth is not in us.

Psalm 51:5 Behold, I was shapen in iniquity; and in sin did my mother conceive me.

I Corinthians 10:12 Wherefore let him that thinketh he standeth take heed lest he fall.

Isaiah 64:6 But we are all as an unclean thing, and all our righteousnesses are as filthy rags; and we all do fade as a leaf; and our iniquities, like the wind, have taken us away.

The other view is that which was mentioned earlier. Islam teaches that they are either sinless or they have not committed any major sins or faults.

The Purpose of a Prophet According to Islam

There are two Arabic words that are the equivalents to the English word prophet. The first is *"rasul,"* which means, "one who is sent." The second is *"nabi,"* which means, "one who carries information and proclaims news from God."

Muslim theologians understand *rasul* to mean one who is sent with a divine scripture. They also understand *nabi* to mean one who is to orally proclaim God's message to a possibly smaller group and will adhere to the scriptures previously sent.

Muslims also believe that God at some time would send a messenger to all people to warn them to turn from their sins, and to obey God just as prophets of earlier times came to warn the Jews.

This warning was given to the prophet through revelations from God. The revelations were later recorded and thus used to be a guide for the people to know how to submit himself or herself to God.

Muslims believe that Muhammad would be recognized as a nabi. According to their teaching and beliefs, Muhammad received new revelations, but also adhered to the previous scriptures. You can see that he used Bible characters and even Bible stories in the Qur'an, but they have been distorted.

Muslims believe that Muhammad was God's choice to warn the Arabic people with the revelations received from the angel Gabriel. Muslims believe the revelations were thus recorded in the form of the Qur'an, which today is the written guide for them, and as they would have everyone to think, for the entire world.

Muslims believe that because of the disobedience of other people (Jews and Christians) to the revelations given to them (the Bible) that God has allowed their written revelations to become altered and changed so that they no longer have a true record.

However, Muslims believe that God has protected the Qur'an and kept it from being corrupted. Thus, they are the only ones to have a true record of the revelations from God. They say that God watched over it because it was His Word, and therefore, would not allow it to be corrupted. Yet, the same Muslim will tell you that at one time the Bible was the Word of God and was pure and true without any corruptions. However, they will turn right around and tell you that it is now corrupted and has been changed by man and is no longer valid as an authority. My question is if the Bible was as they say God's Word, and as they now say the Qur'an is God's Word, why did God keep the Qur'an pure when He could not manage to keep the Bible pure and uncorrupted?

We will look later in the Qur'an and see that the Qur'an still refers to the Bible as the authority, and that even the Qur'an is to be checked by the Bible.

The Message of the Prophet

Muslims believe that in the beginning all prophets preached the same message. The message that was preached by all was that of submission to the divine will. The true prophet invites his people to worship the One and true God.

Muslims believe that what sets Muhammad's message apart from all others was the fact that his was the last and final word from God to humankind. They also believe that it was put into a perfectly written form and preserved without error. Basically they take the same stand on the Qur'an that we Christians take on the Bible, that it is God's Word without error, and that it has been preserved forever.

Muhammad even in his message declared that he was the "Seal of the Prophets." This is stated in the Qur'an.

> *Surah 33:40 Muhammad is not the father of any of your men, but (he is) the Messenger of Allah, and the Seal of the Prophets: and Allah has full knowledge of all things.*

Islam's View of Jesus as Prophet

The Qur'an does not deny Jesus but rather teaches that Jesus was a prophet. However, the Qur'an does deny that Jesus was God in the flesh. Jesus is mentioned either by name or implication in 93 verses in 15 different surahs a total of 97 times.

The title Christ is used nine times, and the name Jesus is used 28 times. Other references to Jesus are as the Word of God, the Spirit of God, the Messenger of God, the son of Mary, a peace from Us, a Mercy from Us, The Speech of Truth, Sign unto Men, and many other types of references.

The Qur'an does recognize Jesus as a great Hebrew prophet, and the name of Jesus appears in every list of prophets along with Abraham.

Notice, surah 4:170-171 names Jesus as an apostle of Allah, His Word, a spirit of God, and the Word of God.

> *Surah 4:170-171 O Mankind! The Messenger hath come to you in truth from Allah. believe in him: It is best for you. But if ye reject Faith, to Allah belong all things in the heavens and on earth: And Allah is All-knowing, All-wise.*
> *171 O People of the Book! Commit no excesses in your religion: Nor say of Allah aught but the truth. Christ Jesus the son of Mary was (no more than) an apostle of Allah, and His Word, which He bestowed on Mary, and a spirit proceeding from Him: so believe in Allah and His apostles. Say not "Trinity": desist: it will be better for you: for Allah is one Allah. Glory be to Him: (far exalted is He) above having a son. To Him belong all things in the heavens and on earth. And enough is Allah as a Disposer of affairs.*

However, even with all the Qur'an has to say about Jesus His greatness and all the titles they give Him, they still deny the death of Jesus on the cross. Read what the Qur'an says concerning this event, and pay close attention to what verse 159 says about His death.

> *Surah 4:157-159 That they said (in boast), "We killed Christ Jesus the son of Mary, the Messenger*

of Allah.;- but they killed him not, nor crucified him, but so it was made to appear to them, and those who differ therein are full of doubts, with no (certain) knowledge, but only conjecture to follow, for of a surety they killed him not:-
158 Nay, Allah raised him up unto Himself; and Allah is Exalted in Power, Wise;-
159 And there is none of the People of the Book but must believe in him before his death; and on the Day of Judgment he will be a witness against them;

Some Muslims do teach that God made someone else to look like Jesus, and this is who was crucified, but Jesus was taken up without passing through death. Some even teach that Jesus did suffer on the cross but was taken up to God before death could take place. Ultimately though all teach and believe that Jesus went to heaven without dying because of this passage. Yet, verse 159 states that the People of the Book must believe in Him before His death, meaning that He has to die. The problem comes from the fact that He went to heaven according to their teaching without dying, and there is no death in heaven. Now, the question that they cannot answer is when is He going to die? This passage causes some great controversy especially when you link this passage to surah 19:33-34.

Surah 19:33-34 "So peace is on me the day I was born, the day that I die, and the day that I shall be raised up to life (again)!"
34 Such (was) Jesus the son of Mary: (it is) a statement of truth, about which they (vainly) dispute.

These verses state that Jesus even said that He would be born, would die, and be raised to life again. There is one of those glimmers of light that God's Word stated would shine out of

100

darkness. They just do not see it until you or I show it to them; but when we do, it is a reality that they will try to deny. They have no grounds to do so. It has come from their book that they say is uncorrupted and that it is total truth.

Now, we will examine another passage from their Qur'an that states that those that follow Jesus are superior to everyone else. It also says that Jesus would be raised up to God depicting a resurrection. Verse 59 could be taken two ways: one that He was merely a man created like Adam from dust, and therefore He would be only human; secondly, <u>God said be (spoken into existence) and He was in the virgin's womb, the miraculous Son of God; which by the way is Bible teaching, and I believe is another one of those rays of light shining forth from darkness.</u>

> *Surah 3:55-59 Behold! Allah said: "O Jesus! I will take thee and raise thee to Myself and clear thee (of the falsehoods) of those who blaspheme; I will make those who follow thee superior to those who reject faith, to the Day of Resurrection: Then shall ye all return unto me, and I will judge between you of the matters wherein ye dispute.*
> *56 As to those who reject faith, I will punish them with terrible agony in this world and in the Hereafter, nor will they have anyone to help.*
> *57 As to those who believe and work righteousness, Allah will pay them (in full) their reward; but Allah loveth not those who do wrong.*
> *58. This is what we rehearse unto thee of the Signs and the Message of Wisdom.*
> *59. The similitude of Jesus before Allah is as that of Adam; He created him from dust, then said to him: "Be". And he was.*

I believe overall this passage, when taken into consideration with the following passage, brings us to the conclusion that Jesus was crucified, buried, and raised to life again just as the Bible account so clearly teaches.

> *Surah 19:33-34 "So peace is on me the day I was born, the day that I die, and the day that I shall be raised up to life (again)!"*
> *34 Such (was) Jesus the son of Mary: (it is) a statement of truth, about which they (vainly) dispute.*

Notice what the translator Abdullah Yusuf Ali had to say in the study notes concerning the statement in surah 4:157 where it said, "Nor crucified him,"

Study note 663 – "The end of the life of Jesus on earth is as much involved in mystery as his birth, and indeed the greater part of his private life except the three main years of his ministry. It is not profitable to discuss the many doubts and conjectures among the early Christian sects and among the Muslim theologians."

They reject the crucifixion of Christ and state this in the notes, but say that is necessary for the Christian teaching of blood sacrifice and vicarious atonement for sins, but then the translator states, "Which is rejected by Islam." Abdullah's notes go on to state, "The Qur'an teaching is that Christ was not crucified nor killed by the Jews, notwithstanding certain apparent circumstances which produced that illusion in the minds of some of His enemies; that disputations, doubts, and conjectures on such matters are vain, and that He was taken up to Allah (See next note)."

I like it when they have to go to another note to try to explain something because in most cases it means that they are not sure what happened. We will see this in the next note 664 that pertains to the statement made in surah 4:158, when it says, "Nay Allah raised him up."

Note 664 – "There is a difference of opinions as to the exact interpretation of this verse…. One school holds that Jesus did not die the usual human death but still lives in the body in heaven, which is the generally accepted Muslim view. Another holds that he did die but not when he was supposed to be crucified, and that being "raised up" unto Allah means that instead of being disgraced as a malefactor, as the Jews intended, he was on the contrary honoured by Allah as His Messenger."

This still has not dealt with the statement made in surah 4:159 of this passage that says, "Before his death." Now to this statement the translator adds another study note in an effort to explain his translation.

665 – "Before his death, Interpreters are not agreed as to the exact meaning."

It is pretty clear that the translator himself is unclear as to the meaning of the statements made concerning the death of Christ. The average Muslim will not have any understanding of them either. Therefore, this is a perfect area for us to show them the Straight Way, Jesus Christ, and the clear teaching of the Bible. God has commanded a lot of light to shine forth out of these passages.

The Bible plainly states that God wants us to know the truth.

II Peter 3:9 The Lord is not slack concerning his promise, as some men count slackness; but is longsuffering to us-ward, not willing that any should perish, but that all should come to repentance.

I Corinthians 14:33 For God is not the author of confusion, but of peace, as in all churches of the saints.

However, Satan is the author of confusion. He is going to do all that he can to keep as many as he can walking in darkness for as long as he can in hopes of leading them to hell.

John 8:44 Ye are of your father the devil, and the lusts of your father ye will do. He was a murderer from the beginning, and abode not in the truth, because there is no truth in him. When he speaketh a lie, he speaketh of his own: for he is a liar, and the father of it.

You will find that the Qur'an over and over makes statements concerning Jesus attacking who He is and His deity. This is not surprising because the devil has confronted Him in the wilderness and failed. So now the devil is going about to lead those that are blinded to the true Word of God further into his grasp in an effort to destroy them eternally.

II Corinthians 4:4 In whom the god of this world hath blinded the minds of them which believe not, lest the light of the glorious gospel of Christ, who is the image of God, should shine unto them.

With this in mind it is easy to see why the following claims or statements are made against Christ in the Qur'an. The devil hates Him and wants to discredit Christ and turn as many as he can from being open to hearing His Word. With this in mind notice some of the claims the Qur'an makes towards Christ.

According to the Qur'an, Christ was no more than an apostle and a servant.

104

Surah 4:171 O People of the Book! Commit no excesses in your religion: Nor say of Allah aught but the truth. Christ Jesus the son of Mary was (no more than) an apostle of Allah, and His Word, which He bestowed on Mary, and a spirit proceeding from Him: so believe in Allah and His apostles. Say not "Trinity": desist: it will be better for you: for Allah is one Allah. Glory be to Him: (far exalted is He) above having a son. To Him belong all things in the heavens and on earth. And enough is Allah as a Disposer of affairs.

Surah 5:75 Christ the son of Mary was no more than an apostle; many were the apostles that passed away before him. His mother was a woman of truth. They had both to eat their (daily) food. See how Allah doth make His signs clear to them; yet see in what ways they are deluded away from the truth!

Surah 43:57-59 When (Jesus) the son of Mary is held up as an example, behold, thy people raise a clamour thereat (in ridicule)!
58 And they say, "Are our gods best, or he?" This they set forth to thee, only by way of disputation: yea, they are a contentious people.
59 He was no more than a servant: We granted Our favour to him, and We made him an example to the Children of Israel.

The Qur'an denies that Jesus was God, which should not be a surprise to a Christian, for the devil hates Him.

Surah 5:17 In blasphemy indeed are those that say that Allah is Christ the son of Mary. Say: "Who then hath the least power against Allah, if His will were to destroy Christ the son of Mary, his mother, and all every - one that is on the earth? For to Allah belongeth the dominion of the heavens and the earth, and all that is between. He createth what He pleaseth. For Allah hath power over all things.

Surah 5:72 They do blaspheme who say: "(Allah) is Christ the son of Mary." But said Christ: "O Children of Israel! worship Allah, my Lord and your Lord." Whoever joins other gods with Allah,- Allah will forbid him the garden, and the Fire will be his abode. There will for the wrong-doers be no one to help.

The Qur'an also denies Jesus as the Son of God.

Surah 9:30-31 The Jews call 'Uzair a son of Allah, and the Christians call Christ the son of Allah. That is a saying from their mouth; (in this) they but imitate what the unbelievers of old used to say. Allah.s curse be on them: how they are deluded away from the Truth!
31 They take their priests and their anchorites to be their lords in derogation of Allah, and (they take as their Lord) Christ the son of Mary; yet they were commanded to worship but One Allah. there is no god but He. Praise and glory to Him: (Far is He) from having the partners they associate (with Him).

Yet in surah 19:19 Jesus is declared by their Qur'an to be the "holy son" making Him to be the Son of God. Even a Muslim will tell you that there is nothing holy apart from God. They say the Qur'an is called holy because it came directly from God and not from man. Therefore, this verse is very useful in showing the

Muslim that Jesus even according to their Qur'an is the Son of God because of the use of the word holy. As a matter of fact Jesus is the only son in the entire Qur'an that has been declared to be the "Holy Son" by the Qur'an.

> *Surah 19:19 He said: "Nay, I am only a messenger from thy Lord, (to announce) to thee the gift of a holy son."*

Before I show surah 19:19 to a Muslim, I like to lay some groundwork. I ask if they have any children; they usually do. Then I ask them why they are their children and not mine. Of course I sometimes have to help them with the answer I am looking for. The answer to the question is that the children are theirs because of who caused the conception. I then ask the question about the word *holy* on the front of their Qur'an. Again, I may have to help them establish the fact that the word *holy* implies that anything that it is attached to belongs to God or that it has come directly from God. Again, note what the verse said concerning the announcement of the birth of Jesus.

> *Surah 19:19 He said: "Nay, I am only a messenger from thy Lord, (to announce) to thee the gift of a holy son."*

Now, to confirm even more so that Jesus is the Son of God, we will look at who caused the conception of Jesus in the virgin's womb. The following is the conversation between Mary and the Angel of God. Notice verse 20-22: she asks how she can have a son when no man has touched her. The angel says that God said it would be easy for him to cause it to happen, and she conceived. So, who caused the conception? According to their Qur'an, their God caused the conception and then put his seal on it declaring Jesus to be His Holy Son.

Surah 19:16-22 Relate in the Book (the story of) Mary, when she withdrew from her family to a place in the East
17 She placed a screen (to screen herself) from them; then We sent to her Our angel, and he appeared before her as a man in all respects.
18 She said: "I seek refuge from thee to (Allah) Most Gracious: (Come not near) if thou dost fear Allah."
19 He said: "Nay, I am only a messenger from thy Lord, (to announce) to thee the gift of a holy son."
20 She said: "How shall I have a son, seeing that no man has touched me, and I am not Unchaste?"
21 He said: "So (it will be): Thy Lord saith, 'That is easy for Me: And (We wish) to appoint him as a Sign unto men and a Mercy from Us': It is a matter (so) decreed."
22 So she conceived him and she retired with him to a remote place.

Most Muslims do not like it, but they cannot deny what it says, even though many will still try to argue that Jesus is not the Son of God. The Holy Spirit of God can now take this beam of light that has shown through and work on their hearts in the days to come. We have gotten a truth through to them from which they cannot escape.

Many Muslims believe that Jesus was sent to the nation of Israel and that His revelation was primarily to reaffirm and revise the mosaic covenant. Notice what it says, "Confirming the Law that had come before him." Also, take note that it says that with Jesus the Gospel was sent, and they do not believe it. The Gospel as we know it being defined as the death, burial, and resurrection of Jesus Christ.

Surah 5:46-47 And in their footsteps We sent Jesus the son of Mary, confirming the Law that had come before him: We sent him the Gospel: therein was guidance and light, and confirmation of the Law that had come before him: a guidance and an admonition to those who fear Allah.
47. Let the people of the Gospel judge by what Allah hath revealed therein. If any do fail to judge by (the light of) what Allah hath revealed, they are (no better than) those who rebel.

Did you notice also that verse 47 said, we that are of the Gospel are to judge by what the Gospel says? It did not say by the Qur'an or the teachings of Islam, but by the Gospel.

Muslims do believe in the virgin birth of Jesus even though their account of it is different in many ways. It can still be used to show them the light.

Surah 3:42-51 Behold! the angels said: "O Mary! Allah hath chosen thee and purified thee- chosen thee above the women of all nations.
43 "O Mary! worship Thy Lord devoutly: Prostrate thyself, and bow down (in prayer) with those who bow down."
44 This is part of the tidings of the things unseen, which We reveal unto thee (O Messenger.) by inspiration: Thou wast not with them when they cast lots with arrows, as to which of them should be charged with the care of Mary: Nor wast thou with them when they disputed (the point).
45 Behold! the angels said: "O Mary! Allah giveth thee glad tidings of a Word from Him: his name will be Christ Jesus, the son of Mary, held in honour in this world and the Hereafter and of (the company

of) those nearest to Allah.
46 "He shall speak to the people in childhood and in maturity. And he shall be (of the company) of the righteous."
47 She said: "O my Lord! How shall I have a son when no man hath touched me?" He said: "Even so: Allah createth what He willeth: When He hath decreed a plan, He but saith to it, 'Be,' and it is!
48 "And Allah will teach him the Book and Wisdom, the Law and the Gospel,
49 "And (appoint him) an apostle to the Children of Israel, (with this message): "'I have come to you, with a Sign from your Lord, in that I make for you out of clay, as it were, the figure of a bird, and breathe into it, and it becomes a bird by Allah.s leave: And I heal those born blind, and the lepers, and I quicken the dead, by Allah.s leave; and I declare to you what ye eat, and what ye store in your houses. Surely therein is a Sign for you if ye did believe;
50 "(I have come to you), to attest the Law which was before me. And to make lawful to you part of what was (Before) forbidden to you; I have come to you with a Sign from your Lord. So fear Allah, and obey me.
51 "It is Allah Who is my Lord and your Lord; then worship Him. This is a Way that is straight.

Did you notice the closing statement, "Way that is straight" and that the word *Way* was capitalized? I believe this is another one of those glimmers of light because Christ is the Way.

There are also some interesting notes by the translator on this passage when it is declared in verse 45 that his name would be Christ Jesus.

Note 386 – "Christ: Greek, Christos = anointed: kings and priests were anointed to symbolize consecration to their office. The Hebrew and Arabic form is Masih."

This Hebrew and Arabic form Masih interestingly enough means Messiah. Even the Qur'an in the study notes has called Christ Jesus the Messiah.

Another very interesting note to the above passage is in reference to verse 46 and the statement that is made there, "In childhood and in maturity."

Note 388 – "The ministry of Jesus lasted only about three years, from 30 to 33 years of his age, when in the eyes of his enemies he was crucified."

Remember, Islam teaches and denies that Jesus was crucified, but here the translator states in note 388 that Jesus was crucified. Not that he appeared to have been and it was an illusion, but he was crucified.

I love to take Muslims to the notes that the translator has given them for further explanation when the verses are not clear. It can be used most of the time to expound the truth of the Bible, God's Word to them.

John 14:6 Jesus saith unto him, I am the way, the truth, and the life: no man cometh unto the Father, but by me.

Another Qur'an passage that deals with the virgin birth is Surah 19.

Surah 19:16-22 Relate in the Book (the story of)

111

Mary, when she withdrew from her family to a place in the East.

17 She placed a screen (to screen herself) from them; then We sent her our angel, and he appeared before her as a man in all respects.

18 She said: "I seek refuge from thee to ((Allah)) Most Gracious: (come not near) if thou dost fear Allah."

19 He said: "Nay, I am only a messenger from thy Lord, (to announce) to thee the gift of a holy son.

20 She said: "How shall I have a son, seeing that no man has touched me, and I am not unchaste?"

21 He said: "So (it will be): Thy Lord saith, 'that is easy for Me: and (We wish) to appoint him as a Sign unto men and a Mercy from Us': It is a matter (so) decreed."

22 So she conceived him, and she retired with him to a remote place.

The Qur'an also teaches many things about Jesus that are not so. One of those things is that Jesus spoke as an infant. He could have, He is God, but there is no such record.

Surah19:29-34 But she pointed to the babe. They said: "How can we talk to one who is a child in the cradle?"

30 He said: "I am indeed a servant of Allah. He hath given me revelation and made me a prophet;

31 "And He hath made me blessed wheresoever I be, and hath enjoined on me Prayer and Charity as long as I live;

32 "(He) hath made me kind to my mother, and not overbearing or miserable;

33 "So peace is on me the day I was born, the day that I die, and the day that I shall be raised up to

112

life (again)"!
34 Such (was) Jesus the son of Mary: (it is) a statement of truth, about which they (vainly) dispute.

My main reason for making mention of this is to emphasize that Jesus is exalted more than anyone else in the Qur'an, and they still will not see Him for who He is. They still deem Muhammad as the greatest in their religion.

Islam's view of Muhammad as the final Prophet
Muhammad is only mentioned five times by name in the Qur'an, which seems strange to me since he is so highly regarded in the religion of Islam.

He was born in A.D. 570 into the Hashim family of the Quraysh tribe in Mecca. His father's name was (Abd-Allah).

Surah 10:94 has a footnote 1475 that makes an interesting statement concerning Muhammad. It says, "Sincere Jews like Abd-Allah." This makes Jews accepting a Muslim as the anti-Christ much more possible. This will be discussed in more detail later. Muhammad's father died before Muhammad's birth, and his mother (Amina) died when he was six. At the age of eight his grandfather (Abd al-Muttalib), who had taken care of him from birth, died also. At this time he was placed in the care of his uncle, Abu Talib.

Muhammad married into a wealthy family at the age of 25. Even though Khadija was 40 when they married, it is said they had a good and happy marriage. They had two sons who died as babies; and then they also had four daughters, one of whom was Fatima, who became the wife of the Caliph Ali, which was Muhammad's cousin.

Muhammad was 40 years of age when he received his first revelation. Nearly another three years passed before he received any more. He began to preach secretly to those with whom he was close and to his family, converting all he could to submit to God. His message was to believe in one sovereign God, resurrection and the last judgment, and to practice charity to the poor and the orphans.

At first the majority of the people rejected his teachings, and his proclaiming to be a prophet. The people of Mecca strongly rejected his teachings that there was but one God, since they were given to the worship of many gods and idols.

In 619 Muhammad's wife Khadija and his uncle Abu Talib both died. Abu Talib, because of his great influence, had been a protector for Muhammad.

During this time there had been several people from Medina who had been making the journey to Mecca to the Kaaba, to worship idols, but were now converted to follow Islam. In 622 Muhammad and about 150 of his followers fled to Medina. About 75 people from Medina had also been converted to Islam. These converts from Medina swore to protect Muhammad as their own kin. In the first 12 to 13 years of Muhammad's teachings, Islam had only grown to a total of about 225 followers.

During this time in Medina Muhammad gained a large following and became very powerful. This was accomplished as a result of situations at that time. Medina was a city that was troubled on every side by many different factions. Muhammad was able to step in and mediate. In A.D. 624 Muhammad and a small group of his followers ambushed a caravan from Mecca. The spoil was divided among the men. This prompted others to help in future raids that were made on trade caravans to Mecca. After that first successful raid the next raid had 300 men taking part. Growth became much more rapid when profit was factored into the equation.

Muhammad did possess great military strategy, and his followers had zeal to fight for Islam. This resulted in continued raids against forces where they were outnumbered three to one, with victory still on their side.

In A.D. 630 Muhammad with an army of more than 10,000 invaded Mecca with almost no resistance. They laid siege against the city, cutting off supplies. After a period of time the city surrendered to Muhammad and his followers. Subsequently a large number of Arabic tribes professed their allegiance to Muhammad.

Muslims may not get too excited if you do not agree with them about Allah, or even if you speak against Allah, but they will if you speak against Muhammad. Muhammad seems to have more devotion than their God, although they will be quick to say that they do not worship Muhammad.

The Qur'an does not say a lot about the life of Muhammad. Yet, the Qur'an is the number one source of authority for the Muslim people. However, the hadiths (recorded sayings and deeds of Muhammad) contain nothing but the remote details of his life. His companions recorded everything that he did or said (supposedly).

I believe the facts of the hadiths contents and their rank as the second most recognized books of authority states the influence that Muhammad had on the followers of Islam. I said "books" because more than one hadith exists and by more than one author containing several variations.

The Five Most Recognized Prophets of Islam

Among all the prophets of Islam there are five that hold the title of ulu'l 'Azm (People of the determination or perseverance). Each is given a descriptive title also.

1. Muhammad - The apostle of God
2. Noah - The preacher of God
3. Abraham - The friend of God
4. Moses - The speaker of God
5. Jesus - The Word of God

David is in the list sometimes, and some Islamic scholars have included Adam as the sixth being the chosen of God. However this is not the general thought in Islam, but you will find the list does vary from time to time depending on who has compiled it. It will consistently have Muhammad, Moses, and Jesus in the list though.

As Muhammad's relationship with the Jews and Christians deteriorated, he referred to Abraham as the founder of Islam and who was neither a Jew nor a Christian according to:

Surah 3:67 Abraham was not a Jew Nor a Christian; But he was true in Faith, And bowed his will to Allah's, (Which is Islam), And he joined not gods with Allah.

It is commonly believed among Islamic scholars that each prophet was given divine scriptures for a particular people. However, it is also commonly believed among Islam followers that the scriptures of Abraham and Noah no longer exist. Also, it is believed that the revelations of Muhammad are the greatest and last of all to be given to mankind.

Followers of Islam will not deny any of the prophets, but they

116

will deny the validity of their scriptures. They do this in two ways:

1. By saying that they no longer exist or they have been destroyed or they have been permanently lost never to be recovered.

2. By being altered or changed. In this way they are contaminated and are no longer valid. Man has rewritten them and changed them in an effort to destroy them.

The writings of Muhammad are believed by followers of Islam to be the only scriptures to have remained unchanged and uncontaminated by man. The main reason for this is because of the belief that he is the final prophet of Islam.

There are several Bible verses that are used by Muslims to try to prove that the Bible has been rewritten and rewritten and that the Bible is no longer valid. This is their justification for the need for the Qur'an to have come into existence. Their argument is not valid in that, the writings and writers that they are saying have been omitted were never a part of the canonicity of the Scriptures, but were only historical writings, writers, or recorders of history, to which the Bible made references. Much like today, many preachers and teachers refer to the writings of Josephus. He was an historian, but he was by no means one of God's chosen to record the Word of God. Read the following Scriptures and you will see the books referenced in these verses are not and have never been a part of the Bible that we hold to be the Word of God. They are described as historical records even in the references that are made to them.

The Book of Jasher:

Joshua 10:13 And the sun stood still, and the moon stayed, until the people had avenged themselves upon their enemies. Is not this written in the book of Jasher? So the sun stood still in the midst of heaven, and hasted not to go down about a whole day.

II Samuel 1:18 (Also he bade them teach the children of Judah the use of the bow: behold, it is written in the book of Jasher.)

The Book of Iddo:

II Chronicles 13:22And the rest of the acts of Abijah, and his ways, and his sayings, are written in the story of the prophet Iddo.

The Book of Nathan, visions of Iddo, and Book of Shemaiah:

II Chronicles 9:29 Now the rest of the acts of Solomon, first and last, are they not written in the book of Nathan the prophet, and in the prophecy of Ahijah the Shilonite, and in the visions of Iddo the seer against Jeroboam the son of Nebat?II Chron. 12:15 - Book of Shemaiah the prophet and Iddo the seer against Jeroboam the son of Nebat?

The Book of Jehu:

II Chronicles 20:34 Now the rest of the acts of Jehoshaphat, first and last, behold, they are written in the book of Jehu the son of Hanani, who is mentioned in the book of the kings of Israel.

Chapter IX
THE KORAN (QUR'AN) OF ISLAM

Qur'an – is from the Arabic word meaning to recite, recitation, or recital.

As you read through the Qur'an, it is evident that Muhammad was very familiar with Jewish and Christian tradition. However, Muhammad believed that both of these groups had departed from their trust or belief in their Scriptures or at least the message God had for them in the Scriptures.

The Qur'an's Origin (Verbally Received by Muhammad)
Some of this has been stated already but needs to be reiterated to fully understand the rest of the material.

It was in the year A.D. 610 while in a cave on Mount Hira just outside of Mecca, Arabia, that Muhammad received his first of many visions. (A.D. 610 –A.D. 632, a period of 22 years, he received 114 revelations) In these first visions he was told by the angel Gabriel that he (Muhammad) was to preach the message that had been entrusted to him.

He received further revelations throughout his lifetime. These were not written down but were recited to those around him at the time. However, after the death of Muhammad the revelations of Muhammad began to differ according to who was telling it. As a result there arose the urgency to record the revelations of Muhammad in writing. Thus, the Qur'an was the collection of those revelations of Muhammad, and they became the accepted Holy Book for the Islamic believers.

The Qur'an's Origin (Written Down In Text)

The Qur'an was not written down except for a few scattered revelations. Muhammad and his followers memorized the majority of the revelations. Not long after the death of Muhammad variations in the revelations began to appear. Also, because of confrontations (jihad or holy wars) that had been taking place, many of those that had the revelations memorized had been killed.

The Caliph Othman or Uthman, who ruled from A.D. 644 to A.D. 656, (12 – 24 years after Muhammad's death), ordered the first official copy to be compiled. It is commonly believed that it was Muhammad's secretary Zayd Ibn Thalbit that did the actual compiling. Muslims believe that God himself has and is watching over his scriptures to insure their pureness.

The companions of Muhammad preserved his revelations mainly by memorizing them, but a few scattered ones were written down during Mohammad's lifetime. Many Muslim scholars believe Muhammad approved these teachings. Later, the materials were combined to form the holy book of the Muslims. It is called the Qur'an, from the Arabic word meaning "recitation." The Caliph Othman sent a copy to the chief mosque in each of the capital cities of the Muslim provinces. Muslims consider the Qur'an to be the words of God Himself, spoken to Muhammad by the angel Gabriel.

Parts of the Qur'an resemble the Bible, the Apocrypha, and the Talmud (customs & traditions). The Qur'an contains many stories about the prophets that appear in the Old Testament. The Qur'an also has stories from the New Testament about Jesus Christ, whom it calls the Word of God.

The Form in Which the Qur'an is Written

The general tone of the book is poetic which is most evident in

120

the earlier surahs or chapters. In these earlier chapters you will find the structure contains short sentences with the rhyming being more apparent. In the later chapters the sentences are much longer, and it is very difficult to determine if the rhyme is intended to indicate the end of a verse.

Each surah or chapter has a title from some significant word in the surah, such as "The Moon," "The Believers," or "The Greeks." The full content of each surah is not indicated by these titles, and the title word may only be mentioned in passing.

The Qur'an is comparable in length to the New Testament. Actually it has less content than the New Testament. The English version is written with the left column in English and the right column in Arabic. Each page will have the translator's footnotes or commentary ranging from being a very brief statement to taking most of the page to explain. The Qur'an therefore appears to be a large book when in reality it is not at all especially when you consider that Islam has this little book as their complete and final authority for life and government.

The Order of the Qur'an's Surahs
The surahs or chapters are not in any type of chronological or logical order. When they were written or when they took place chronologically is not indicated in or by their order. They were written during three periods of time and from two locations, Mecca and Medina. They are not divided by these periods of time or locations either.

With the exception of the first surah or chapter (7 verses), which is a short introductory prayer, the remaining surahs are arranged generally according to their length, but that is not always the case. Surah 2 (286 verses) is the longest of the 114 surahs and they get shorter towards the end of the book, but that does not hold true all the way, as there are variations even to that rule.

121

Eighty-six of the surahs were revealed during the Mecca period, and twenty-eight were revealed at Medina. The Mecca period is divided into two parts. The first Mecca period was from A.D. 610 – A.D. 622, when Muhammad fled from Mecca to Medina. The second period was from A.D. 630 – A.D. 632, which was the time when Muhammad returned with an army of more than 10,000 and conquered Mecca, controlling it until his death in A.D. 632. The Medina period yielded twenty-eight surahs from A.D. 622 – A.D. 630.

Most of the longer surahs were the later revelations, while most of the shorter surahs were the earlier revelations. Therefore, if there is any order, it is reversed. Again, that does not always hold true either, but it is the case the majority of the time.

Each surah also opens with the statement, "In the name of Allah, Most Gracious, Most Merciful." The Qur'an is divided into divisions for daily reading so that it can be read through every month. Muslims are encouraged to read through their Qur'an monthly, and many devout Muslims do read it monthly.

The Qur'an's Purpose
The Qur'an was revealed to Muhammad in Arabic so that the Arabic-speaking people would be provided with a holy book in their own language which would be comparable to the Scriptures of Judaism and Christianity.

It was to bring the Arabic people back to worship the one true God. It was intended to bring them out of their idolatry that was so prevalent in the early days of Muhammad's life and even at the time when he received his first supposed revelation. It was also to be their guide in all things private and public. Muslims believe this book lays down the best rules for social life, commerce, economics, marriage, inheritance, penal laws, and international conduct. It was to be the final authority in all matters superseding all other previous divine revelations.

Muslims also believe that the "sending down" of the Qur'an is the perfection of religion and the completion of God's favor to humanity. They say that since the Qur'an recognizes other prophets and scriptures which were before it that it must be the crowning or completion of religion. However, the Islamic community in contradiction to their own teaching, does not say that the Qur'an backs up the other scriptures, but rather replaces them, and has thus become the only true authority.

According to Islamic teaching those who recognize the Qur'an as the ultimate authority and truth show themselves to be true believers, while those who reject it prove themselves to be unbelievers no matter what name they call themselves.

Arguments Supporting the Qur'an's Existence
The Islamic community argues that the Qur'an because of its miraculous content and origin must be from God. There are several reasons for their arguments for the Qur'an.

1. Islam says that Muhammad was illiterate and that it would have been impossible for him to write such a masterpiece with its superb literary form.

   Surah 7:157a, Those who follow the Messenger, The unlettered prophet, Whom they find mentioned In their own (Scriptures) In the Law and the Gospel For he commands them What is just and forbids them What is evil; ...

The fact is that Muhammad never wrote any of the Qur'an because he was illiterate, and those in Islam believe this. In fact it was not written down until after his death, and even then those that

123

were his friends gave from memory the portions that they knew. His followers were not illiterate, or they are not recorded as being so. Therefore, one might ask, where is the miracle of it being written by an illiterate. The one that was supposed to be illiterate (Muhammad) did not write anything.

2. Islam says that any mere creature could not have written it.

> *Surah 10:37 This Qur'an is not such As can be produced By other then Allah; On the contrary it is A confirmation of (revelations) That went before it, And a fuller explanation Of the Book -- wherein There is no doubt -- From the Lord of the Worlds.*

Islam yet today believes that their challenge (Muslims claim to have put forth a challenge to anyone to match the Qur'an in its content and writing) has never been matched in its writing. Muslims say that no book has ever matched the Qur'an in diction, style, rhetorical thoughts, and soundness of laws and regulations to shape the destinies of mankind. They still claim that it is unmatched in its quality. However, they refuse to consider anything else seriously.

3. Islam also claims that the fact that the Qur'an has been kept from any textual corruption is another evidence of its divine existence.

In answer to this we will glance through the front of the Qur'an. (This is the Qur'an's English translation by Abdulla Yusif Ali) In the very front is a page that has a heading "An Appeal To Our Readers." This is not exaggerated but written as it appears, "We will greatly appreciate it if our readers inform us of any typographical errors that may have escaped our proofreaders in the translation and commentary of this edition." This statement alone

124

would cause me and should cause anyone else to have serious problems reading it with an eternal destination in mind.

Again this is the "Abdullah Yusuf Ali" translation that I am using which is a widely accepted English translation. As a matter of fact it is probably the most used translation in English in the world. I have even asked Muslims outside the United States, and they have confirmed that it is a commonly used translation. In countries where the Arabic language is not the common language, English is the language that is used in the Qur'an almost every time.

Amana Corporation located in Brentwood, Maryland, publishes this Qur'an with Abdullah Yusuf Ali's translation and notes. On the publishing page it also states that this is the New Revised (Fifth) Edition Published as the Holy Qur'an 1989. It also says that it is the New Edition with revised translation and commentary. I state this because Muslims are very quick to find fault with the Bible saying it has been rewritten and rewritten which has allowed it to be changed and no longer valid. Yet, the front of their Qur'an declares that it has had that very thing happen to it. As a matter of fact based on what is printed on those opening pages, it has been revised (which means changed) five times, since it is the Fifth Edition. My Bible does not declare such a thing. Even though it has been translated into English, it has retained one hundred percent accuracy with the original language. Muslims say that is why they have the Arabic written on the right side of the page across from the English, and that the Arabic has never changed. The problem for most Muslims is that they cannot read Arabic and are therefore totally dependent upon the English translation for their understanding of the Qur'an.

The next page titled Publisher's Note states at the bottom of the page, "In this edition we have removed the words "New Revised Edition" to avoid any misconception by our non-Muslim readers. This is therefore a new edition of the English meaning of the Holy Qur'an with revised translation and commentary." They say this as though a Muslim should not be bothered by the fact of the revisions but that only non-Muslims would be bothered. What are they trying to hide?

Now, onto the "Preface To The New Edition," midway down the first page it says, "A. Yusuf Ali was quick to point out that there can be no absolute or perfect translation of the Qur'an and, at best, only an interpretation of its understood meaning can be offered. Probably he never envisaged how universal his work would someday become, for he was primarily attempting to explain his understanding of the Qur'an to his fellow countrymen – both Muslim and non-Muslim alike. Therefore, he was apt to occasionally use references which could not be easily appreciated outside the milieu of the Indian subcontinent."

In other words, you might need to understand Indian culture and traditions to understand what was meant for the Arabic people. However, this is not the best part of the preface, as you will see in the following quotes.

Abdullah Yusuf Ali said, "Revisions have been made in both the content and form of the original work. Where necessary, the content has been brought up-to-date and within the current understanding and interpretation of the Qur'an." He goes on to say, "There were also a few instances in which certain portions of the materials were deleted either due to its out-datedness or due to its proneness to misinterpretation."

Muslims certainly do not like to have things like this pointed out, but it is an eye opener. Muslims are placing their confidence in a man to help them understand a book that he himself says is out of date and needed to be changed and brought up to date. He even deleted what he thought did not pertain to those for whom it was written. It sounds to me like he placed himself in a position as God and Judge.

Abdullah Yusuf Ali said, "In translating the Text I have aired no views of my own, but followed the received Commentators. Where they differ among themselves, I have had to choose what appeared to me to be the most reasonable opinion from all points of view. Where it is a question merely of words, I have not considered the question important enough to discuss in the Notes, but where it is a question of substance, I hope adequate explanations will be found in the Notes. In some instances I have departed from the literal translation in order to express the spirit of the original better in English. I have explained the literal meaning in the Notes. In choosing an English word for an Arabic word, a translator necessarily exercises his own judgment and may be unconsciously expressing a point of view, but that is inevitable."

I think that it is pretty obvious that even the translator himself, in the things that he has acknowledged about his own work, is telling the reader if he will listen, that it has been rewritten and rewritten and that it is merely expressing one man's point of view. I love for the Muslim to ask, "What do the notes say?" as I am dealing with them with these passages from the Qur'an, and they cannot answer my questions. With the notes you can show contradictions to their teaching and beliefs, as we have already demonstrated.

This is following the plan that I laid out earlier of removing the ruble or stuff that is in the way of building. These things are destroying their faith in the Qur'an. We are drawing them to the truth of the Bible. With each of the things we share that discredits the Qur'an, we are getting to share a truth of God's Word, and it is validated more and more with each instance. Their own authority, the Qur'an, is shaking their foundations. Now the Holy Spirit is taking the truths that we have shared and is beginning to create doubts about their religion.

4. Islam also argues that the changed lives and cultures are a sure proof of its origin and existence. There is no doubt that the Qur'an is responsible for the changed lives and cultures of many nations, but they are not changes that have been for the good of the people. History proves this to be true.

5. Islam also argues that the Qur'an is God's word based on the fact that there are no contradictions in it at all. We have already seen many contradictions in it, and we will see many more. We will look at some more in the last section of the course.

6. Islam also argues that the prophetic content of the Qur'an proves it is of God. Yet, how can Islam lay claim to the prophetic content of any prediction that has come true that was in the pages of the Qur'an? I say this because if it is a prediction that has come true, you can be assured that it was in the pages of the Bible centuries before. So, where should credit for the predictions be given, to the Qur'an or the Bible?

7. Islam argues that the Qur'an's accuracy is proof of its Divine origin. They say that it would have been impossible for someone in the seventh century (Muhammad) to write on topics that did not pertain to that time period, especially with the accuracy that the Qur'an has. Once again, the Muslim is crediting the Qur'an with accuracy that it has been copied or stolen from the Bible.

It has already been established in the course that Muhammad had a good knowledge of the Bible and that much of the Qur'an is the Bible retold. Muhammad's knowledge of the Bible shows a strong doubt that he was illiterate, and also shows where he got at least some of his revelations of prophesy.

Themes That Carry Through The Qur'an

The main emphasis of the book is on the oneness of Allah in contrast to the multiplicity of gods worshipped by the Arabs. The Qur'an denounces the multiplicity of gods being worshiped by the Arabs as powerless idols who will be unable to help unbelievers on the Day of Judgment.

Other themes that carry through the pages of the Qur'an are those of the resurrection from the dead, angels, devils, heaven, and hell.

Chapter X
THE GOD (ALLAH) OF ISLAM

Islam's Title for God (Allah)

The origin of the word Allah is simply the Arabic word for God. As we have already discussed earlier in the course, it was even used in pre-Islamic literature. Even Arabic Christians use the word Allah when they speak of God. However, Islamists that use the word Allah are definitely not talking about the same God that the Christians are when they use the word Allah. Both are speaking of God the Creator of all things, but differ significantly beyond this point.

Muhammad was faced with a great problem as he sought to find a name for the God of his new revelations, since he was trying to bring his people to or back to a worship of one God and not many gods as they were already involved in. So, in his search for a name he came to the name Allah, which was also used by the Christians throughout Arabia. Muhammad's father's name was Abd-Allah which meant "Slave of God." I am sure that this also had a bearing on his choice for the name he would use for the God of Islam.

The Ninety-nine Names of God

Even though Islam states vehemently that there is but one God, they have 99 names for him. They take the names or at least the meaning of the names from different verses in the Qur'an, even though the name may not be mentioned in the verses. They believe these names describe their God and His attributes.

Islam's 99 Names of Allah

1. Allah, the Name that is above every name
2. al-Awwal, the First, who was before the beginning (57:3)
3. al-Akhir, the Last, who will still be after all has ended (57:3)
4. al-Badi, the Contriver, who contrived the whole art of creation (2:117)
5. al-Bari, the Maker, from whose hand we all come (59:24)
6. al-Barr, the Beneficent, whose liberality appears in all his works (52:28)
7. al-Basir, the Observant, who sees and hears all things (57:3)
8. al-Basit, the Spreader, who extends his mercy to whom he wills (13:26)
9. al-Batin, the Inner, who is immanent in all things (57:3)
10. al-Baith, the Raiser, who will raise up a witness from each community (6:89, 91)
11. al-Baqi, the Enduring, who is better and more enduring (20:73, 75)
12. al-Tawwab, the Relenting, who relented toward Adam and relents to all his descendants (2:37)
13. al-Jabbar, the Mighty One, whose might and power are absolute (59:23)
14. al-Jalil, the Majestic, mighty and majestic is he
15. al-Jami, the Gatherer, who gathers all men to an appointed Day (3:9)
16. al-Hasib, the Accounter, who is sufficient as a reckoner (4:6-7)
17. al-Hafiz, the Guardian, who keeps watch over everything (11:57, 60)
18. al-Haqq, the Truth (20:114)

19. al-Hakem, the Judge, who gives judgment among his servants (40:48, 51)
20. al-Hakim, the Wise, who is both wise and well informed (6:18)
21. al-Halim, the Kindly, who is both forgiving and kindly disposed (2:225)
22. al-Hamid, the Praiseworthy, to whom all praise is due (2:267, 270)
23. al-Hayy, the Living, who is the source of all life (20:111)
24. al-Khabir, the Well-Informed, who is both wise and well informed (6:18)
25. al-Khafid, the Humbler, who humbles some while he exalts others (cf 56:3)
26. al-Khaliq, the Creator, who has created all things that are (13:16-17)
27. al-Dhul-Jalal wal-Ikram, Lord of Majesty and Honor (55:27)
28. ar-Rauf, the Gentle, who is compassionate toward his people (2:143)
29. ar-Rahman, the Merciful, the most merciful of those who show mercy (1:3, 12:64)
30. ar-Rahim, the Compassionate, who is gentle and full of compassion (1:3, 2:143)
31. ar-Razzaq, the Provider, who provides but asks no provision (51:57-58)
32. ar-Rashid, the Guide, who leads believers in the right-minded way (11:87, 89)
33. ar-Rafi, the Exalter, who exalts some while he humbles others (6:83)
34. ar- Raqib, the Watcher, who keeps watch over his creation (5:117)
35. as-Salam, the Peace-Maker, whose name is Peace (59:23)
36. as-Sami, the Hearer, who sees and hears all

things (17:1)
37. ash-Shakur, the Grateful, who graciously accepts the service of his people (64:17)
38. ash-Shahid, the Witness, who is witness to all things (5:117)
39. as-Sabur, the Forebearing, who has great patience with his people
40. as-Samad, the Eternal, who begets not and is not begotten (112:2)
41. ad-Darr, the Afflicter, who sends affliction as well as blessing (48:11)
42. az-Zahir, the Outer, who is without as within (47:3)
43. al-Adl, the Just, whose word is perfect in veracity and justice (6:115)
44. al-Aziz, the Sublime, mighty in his sublime sovereignty (59:23)
45. al-Azim, the Mighty, he who is above all is high and mighty (2:255-256)
46. al-Afuw, the Pardoner, ever ready to forgive his servants (4:99-100)
47. al-Alim, the Knowing One, who is well aware of everything (2:29)
48. al-Ali, the High One, he who is high and mighty (2:255-256)
49. al-Ghafur, the Forgiving, who is both forgiving and well disposed (2:235)
50. al-Ghaffar, the Pardoning, ever ready to pardon and forgive (71:10)
51. al-Ghani, the Rich, since it is he who possesses all things (2:267, 270)
52. al-Fattah, the Opener, who clears and opens up the way (34:26)
53. al-Qabid, the Seizer, who both holds tight and opened handed (2:245-246)

54. al-Qadir, the Able, who has power to do what he pleases (17:99, 101)
55. al-Quddus, the Most Holy One, to whom all in heaven and on earth ascribe holiness (62:1)
56. al-Qahhar, the All-Victorious, who overcomes all (13:16-17)
57. al-Qawi, the Strong, sublime in his strength and his power (13:19)
58. al-Qayyum, the Self-Subsistent, eternally existing in and for himself alone (3:2)
59. al-Kabir, the Great One, who is both high and great (22:62)
60. al-Karim, the Munificent, who is not only rich but generous (27:40)
61. al-Latif, the Gracious, whose grace extends to all his servants (42:19)
62. al-Mutaakhkhir, the Defender, who when he wills defers punishment (14:42-43)
63. al-Mumin, the Faithful, who grants security to all (59:23)
64. al-Mutaali, the Self-Exalted, who has set himself high above all (13:9-10)
65. al-Mutakabbir, the Proud, whose pride is in his works (59:23)
66. al-Matin, the Firm, firm in his possession of strength (51:58)
67. al-Mubdi, the Originator, who both originates and restores (85:13)
68. al-Mujib, the Answerer, who responds when his servants call (11:61, 64)
69. al-Majid, the Glorious, praiseworthy and glorious is he (11:73, 76)
70. al-Muhsi, the Computer, who has counted and numbered all things (19:94)
71. al-Muhyi, the Quickener, who quickens and

brings to life the dead (30:50)

72. al-Mudhill, the Abaser, who raises to honor or abases whom he will (3:26)
73. al-Muzil, the Separator, who will separate men from the false gods they vainly worship (10:28-29)
74. al-Musawwir, the Fashioner, who fashions his creatures how he pleases (59:24)
75. al-Muid, the Restorer, who both originates and restores (85:13)
76. al-Muizz, the Honorer, who honors or abases whom he will (3:26)
77. al-Muti, the Giver, from whose hand comes all good things (20:50, 52)
78. al-Mughni, the Enricher, who enriches men from his bounty (9:74-75)
79. al-Muqit, the Well-Furnished, provided with power over all things (4:85, 87)
80. al-Muqtadir, he who prevails, having evil men in his powerful grip (54:42)
81. al-Muqaddim, the Bringer-Forward, who sends his promises on ahead (50:28)
82. al-Muqsit, the Observer of Justice, who will set up the balances with justice (21:47-48)
83. al-Malik, the King, who is king of kings (59:23)
84. Malik al-Mulk, Possessor of the Kingdom, who grants sovereignty to whom he will (3:26)
85. al-Mumit, he who causes to die, just as he causes to live (15:23)
86. al-Muntaqim, the Avenger, who wreaks vengeance on sinners and succors the believers (30:47)
87. al-Muhaimin, the Preserver, whose watchful care is over all (59:23)

88. an-Nasir, the Helper, and sufficient as a helper is he 94:45, 47)

89. an-nur, The Light, Illuminating both earth and heaven (24:35)

90. al-Hadi, the Guide, who leads believers in the straight oath (22:54)

91. al-Wahed, the One, unique in his Divine sovereignty (13:16-17)

92. al-Wahid, the Unique, who alone has created (74:11)

93. al-Wadud, the Loving, compassionate and loving to his servants (11:90, 92)

94. al-Warith, the Inheritor, unto whom all things will return (19:40-41)

95. al-Wasi, the Wide-Reaching, whose bounty reaches all (2:268, 271)

96. al-Wakil, the Administrator, who has charge of everything (6:102)

97. al-Waliy, the Patron, and a sufficient patron is he (4:45, 47)

98. al-Wali, the Safeguard, other than whom men have no sure guard (13:11-12)

99. al-Whhab, the Liberal Giver, who gives freely of his bounty (3:8)

Islam claims or boasts that there are no other sacred or non-sacred books outside of the Qur'an that can show in number or meaning the attributes of God.

Islam says that because God is the one that wills all things he does not have to conform to any particular one. As the one that wills (the willer) all things that are, he may be recognized by the description of the name but does not have to essentially conform to it according to their teaching. In other words God does not have to live up to the names that are attributed to him. They say he is God and he can do as he wills. This sure does not line up with the God we serve, the God of the Bible.

> *Titus 1:2 In hope of eternal life, which God, that cannot lie, promised before the world began;*

> *Hebrews 4:15 For we have not an high priest which cannot be touched with the feeling of our infirmities; but was in all points tempted like as we are, yet without sin.*

> *James 1:13 Let no man say when he is tempted, I am tempted of God: for God cannot be tempted with evil, neither tempteth he any man:*

I choose the God of the Bible, and I have seen many of them do the same after they have been led through much of the materials that we are covering. When we have thoroughly removed the rubbish and cleared the way for truth, they will begin to see as God opens their eyes to His Wonderful Word.

God's Oneness in Islam
Islam is definitely a Monotheistic Religion as is Christianity and Judaism.

Islam, however, denies the Triune God saying that God (Allah) has no partners, equals, and has begotten no one. Yet the Qur'an uses the plurals "We and Us" over and over again. They deny but cannot really explain these words using pluralities found throughout the Qur'an. They try to explain the plural words used in references to God as happening during translation. However, anyone that knows anything about translation knows that singular does not become plural, and plural does not become singular in translating text. Just as genders remain the same in translation, so does plurality.

They are very dogmatic about the Oneness of God (Allah), and are opposed to anyone that refuses to recognize God (Allah) the same as they do.

The Sovereignty of God

Islam definitely does not deny the sovereignty of God. They believe that he is in absolute sovereign control of all things. Since he is the one that wills all things, nothing can take place without his initiating it and controlling it from start to finish. They believe that God controls who chooses to follow him and who chooses not to follow him. God chooses who will be in heaven and who will be in hell. According to their belief about sovereignty, man has absolutely no choice in the matter.

Since Islam believes that God has no equals or partners, he alone makes all decisions and does so without consulting anyone.

Islam's View Of God's Will For Mankind

Let's look at what the Qur'an has to say about God's (Allah's) will for man.

Surah 9:51 Say: "Nothing will happen to us Except what Allah has decreed For us: He is our Protector": And on Allah let the Believers Put their trust."

Surah 32:13 If we had so willed, We could have certainly brought Every Soul its true guidance: But the Word from Me Will come true, "I will Fill Hell with Jinns And men all together.

According to this last verse their God is definitely not the same as the God of our Bible, for their God is not willing to bring true guidance to every soul. What a sad thought that multitudes would choose to follow a God like this.

> *II Peter 3:9 The Lord is not slack concerning his promise, as some men count slackness; but is longsuffering to us-ward, not willing that any should perish, but that all should come to repentance.*

I am so thankful that my God is not willing that any should perish, but that He desires all to come to repentance.

Islam's popular belief is that not only can God do anything, but also that it is God who is the One that actually does everything.

Example from a Muslim theologian: When a man writes, he does it because Allah has created in the man's mind the will to write. It is Allah who gives the power to write, and it is also Allah that puts the hand in motion to do the writing. Allah controls the hand, the pen, and what appears on the paper.

> *Surah 37:94-96 Then came (the worshippers) With hurried steps, And faced (him). He said: "Worship ye That which ye have (Yourselves) carved? "But Allah has created you And your handiwork!"*

The above verse according to their own beliefs tells us that Allah created idols, not that he allowed them to be created, but that he did the creating.

Worshipping idols is sin, and so is creating them, and if you were to ask a Muslim if forcing someone to worship an idol would be a sin, he would quickly admit that it would be a sin. The previous verse declared that their God created the idol, and evidently forced them to worship the idols also. So, according to their Qur'an, their God sinned. Their God is about to judge them for worshipping an idol, but they can only do as he wills for them to do. How can that be a fair or right act of their God?

> *Surah 81:29 But ye shall not will Except as Allah wills – The Cherisher of the Worlds.*

It is believed by most Islamists that Allah alone is active, and everything else is passive. It is evident that God's will for man, according to the Qur'an and Islamic teaching, is pretty clear. If God does not will you to do good or to find favor in his sight, then you are doomed to a life of wrong-doing and eternal hell. Seeing how God is the one that wills all things, it is in his hands what you will do.

Islam's View of God's Mercy

> *Surah 6:12 He hath inscribed For Himself (the rule of) Mercy.*

> *Surah 7:156 And ordain for us That which is good, In this Life And in the Hereafter: For we have turned unto Thee." He said, "With My Punishment I visit whom I will; But My Mercy extendeth To all things. That (Mercy) I shall ordain for those Who do right, and practise Regular charity, and those Who believe in Our Signs-*

Basically the rule God has for mercy according to Islam is that if he wants to show mercy he will show mercy, but if he does not want to he is not obligated in any way to show mercy. The Qur'an says that if you repent God will show mercy, but you cannot repent if God does not put in you the desire to repent, for he is the one that governs the will of man. The Qur'an teaches that God's mercy is given to those that do good works but not to those that do evil works. However, man cannot do good works unless God wills him to do good works.

Man cannot even love God unless God puts in man the will to love God. Man has no choice in the matter. Man is merely a puppet on a string with God making all the decisions for him. Man cannot even seek to know God or know about him unless God puts this will in man's mind.

According to Webster, Mercy means: a refraining from harming or punishing offenders, enemies, etc.; kindness in excess of what may be expected.

A disposition to forgive or be kind.
The power to forgive or be kind; clemency.
Kind or compassionate treatment.

I believe it is easy to see the definition of mercy is not the same in the doctrine of Islam. They claim that Allah is a merciful God, but only to those to whom he chooses to be merciful. This is not true mercy, not as we see it in the Bible.

You cannot get away from John 3:16, which shows God's mercy demonstrated to the extreme. It is not for the deserving, because none deserve, but it is for the entire world that whosoever crowd?

> *John 3:16 For God so loved the world, that he gave his only begotten Son, that whosoever believeth in him should not perish, but have everlasting life.*
>
> *Lamentations 3:22-23 It is of the LORD'S mercies that we are not consumed, because his compassions fail not.*
> *23 They are new every morning: great is thy faithfulness.*

Chapter XI
THE ANGELS OF ISLAM

As we have already seen, Islam definitely believes in angels. The belief in angels is one of the five Doctrinal Pillars of their faith. Who are the angels, and what do they believe about them? They are broken down into three groups with each group having their own duties to perform.

The Four Archangels of Islam

There are four Archangels recognized in the religion of Islam. They are Gabriel, Michael, Israfil, and Izra'il. The first two Michael and Gabriel are mentioned in the Bible with Michael being referred to as the archangel. The last two are only found in the Qur'an and the teachings of the religion of Islam.

Recording or Guardian Angels

Surah 50:17-18 Behold, two (guardian angels) Appointed to learn (his doings) Learn (and note them), One sitting on the right And one on the left. 18 Not a word does he Utter but there is a sentinel by him, Ready (to note it).

It is believed that these angels also attend meetings of prayer and record the prayers. Some even believe that there is a day shift of angels and a night shift of angels.

Muslims believe that the number of these types of angels is numberless.

Islam also believes that there are angels that are to keep watch over the believers of Allah. They are to see that no harm comes to them. However, as we saw earlier, how could they be harmed unless God willed it? Islam also believes that it will be angels that will witness against man on the Day of Judgment. It is also strongly believed by Muslims that angels have aided them in the day of battle.

Receiving Angels and Errand Angels

Surah 79:1-5 By the (angels) Who tear out (The souls of the wicked) With violence;
2 By those who gently Draw out (the souls Of the blessed);
3 And by those who glide Along (on errands of mercy),
4 Then press forward As in a race,
5 Then arrange to do (The Commands of their Lord)—

Islam believes that when a person dies that there are appointed angels that come to remove the soul from the body. They then usher that soul to either heaven or hell depending on if the person was a believer or not. Also as the passage stated there are angels that are God's errand runners. They do whatever God bids them to do.

Satan

Satan is also known as Iblis in the Islamic religion and in the writings of Islam. The Qur'an uses both of these titles for Satan and others as well, like deceiver, chief deceiver and many more. However, Iblis and Satan are the two most popular titles.

Surah 7:11 It is We Who created you And gave you shape; Then We bade the angels Bow down to

143

Adam, and they Bowed down; not so Iblis; He refused to be of those Who bow down.

According to this and many other passages from the Qur'an, Satan was one of the angels. This is very important to note because Islam teaches that an angel cannot sin. Sin concerning the angels is not the same as sin concerning the prophets. The prophets were allowed to have minor sins or faults, but this is not the case with the angels; they were not allowed this tolerance.

So when Satan refused to bow down with all the other angels, before Adam, God's creation, he sinned and was cast out of heaven.

Surah 15:30-35 So the Angels prostrated themselves, All of them together:
31 Not so Iblis: he refused to be Among those who prostrated themselves.
32 Allah said: "O Iblis! What is your reason For not being among those Who prostrate themselves?"
33 Iblis said,"I am not one To prostrate myself to man, Whom Thou didst create From sounding clay, from mud Moulded into shape."
34 (Allah) said, "Then get thee out From here: for thou art Rejected, accursed.
35 "And the Curse shall be On thee till the Day of Judgement."

Surah 17:61-64 tells of the same account, and even how that after Satan was cast out or rejected, God gave him permission to get revenge on man whom God had created.

Surah 17:61-64 Behold! We said to the angels: "Bow down unto Adam": They bowed down except Iblis: He said, "Shall I bow down to one whom

144

Thou didst create from clay? "
62 He said, "Seest Thou? This is the one whom
Thou hast honored above me! If Thou wilt but
respite me to the Day of Judgment, I will surely
bring his descendants under my sway—all but a
few!"
63 (Allah) said: "Go thy way; if any of them follow
thee, verily Hell will be the recompense of you (all)
—an ample recompense.
64 "Lead to destruction those whom thou canst
among them, with thy (seductive) voice; make
assaults on them with thy cavalry and thy infantry;
mutually share with them wealth and children; and
make promises to them." But Satan promises them
nothing but deceit. "

There is one verse in the entire Qur'an that says that Satan was a Jinn. Surah 18:50 states that Satan or Iblis was one of the Jinn, and Muslims use this trying to justify why he did not bow down when he was commanded to do so. However, this is the only reference that would classify him as Jinn. All other Qur'an accounts classify him plainly as an angel, which creates a major problem in their doctrine concerning angels. If you remember, their teachings state very plainly the fact that an angel cannot sin. If you remember the sections on dealing with the prophets and their sin, we saw Muslims believed that the prophets just did not do anything really bad. This time it is different, for they believe that it is impossible for an angel to sin, and Satan according to their teaching sinned and refused to bow down when God commanded him to do so.

Surah 38:71-85 is another account that shows that Satan was an angel. If he was not, then why did God ask why he refused to bow down?

Surah 38:71-85 Behold, thy Lord said to the angels: "I am about to create man from clay:
72 "When I have fashioned him (in due proportion) and breathed into him of My spirit, fall ye down in obeisance unto him."
73 So the angels prostrated themselves, all of them together:
74 Not so Iblis: He was haughty, and became one of those who reject Faith.
75 (Allah) said: "O Iblis! What prevents thee from prostrating thyself to one whom I have created with My hands? Art thou haughty? Or art thou one of the high (and mighty) ones?"
76 (Iblis) said: "I am better than he: Thou createdst me from fire and him thou createdst from clay."
77 (Allah) said: "Then get thee out from here: For thou art rejected, accursed.
78 "And My Curse shall be on thee till the Day of Judgment."
79 (Iblis) said: "O my Lord! Give me then respite till the Day the (dead) are raised."
80 (Allah) said: "Respite then is granted thee—
81 "Till the Day of the Time Appointed."
82 (Iblis) said: "Then by Thy Power, I will put them all in the wrong, —
83 "Except Thy Servants amongst them, sincere and purified (by Thy grace)."
84 (Allah) said: "Then it is just and fitting—and I say what is just and fitting—
85 "That I will certainly fill Hell with thee and those that follow thee. —Every one."

Jinn of Islam

There is a lot of uncertainty concerning Jinn. However, it is commonly believed among the Islamic community that they are powerful, intelligent, and independent creatures that possess the right or freedom to make choices. As a result of their choices, there are some that are good and some that are evil.

Surah 72 is devoted to the Jinn. In this surah, you will see that some have listened to the reciting of the Qur'an and have become believers in Allah. Others have continued to reject and are doomed to hell, working evil in this world. Those Jinn that have believed in this surah speak out against those that believe not.

The Role or Activities of Archangels

1. Gabriel: in Islam is the angel of revelation and is recognized by many Muslims as the Holy Spirit. Gabriel is believed to have dictated the Qur'an to Muhammad.

2. Michael: in Islam is the angel of providence, preparing Islam's way into the future. They also see or believe Michael to be the guardian of the Jews.

3. Israfil: in Islam is believed to be the one that will call everyone forth in the resurrection. Therefore, he is known as the summoner to resurrection.

4. Izra'il: in Islam is believed to be the death angel.

Of the four Gabriel holds the most prominent position because of his delivering the Divine Revelation.

> *Surah 2:97-98 "Say: Whoever is an enemy To Gabriel -- for he brings down The (revelation) to thy heart By Allah's will, a confirmation Of what went before. And guidance and glad tidings For those who believe—*
> *98 Whoever is an enemy to Allah And His angels and prophets, To Gabriel and Michael -- Lo! Allah*

is an enemy to those Who reject Faith."

The Role or Activities of Satan

Satan's chief role is as the deceiver of mankind. According to theologians of Islam, ever since Allah asked him to bow down before Adam, Satan has been determined to deceive man and cause him to fall. Satan looks at man as being the one that caused his fall, and he intends to get vengeance against man.

Surah 35:5 O men! certainly The promise of Allah Is true. Let not then This present life deceive you, Nor let the Chief Deceiver Deceive you about Allah.

Surah 4:120 Satan makes them promises, And creates in them false desires; But Satan's promises Are nothing but deception.

Surah 5:91 Satan's plan is (but) To excite enmity and hatred Between you, with intoxicants And gambling, and hinder you From the remembrance Of Allah, and from prayer: Will ye not then abstain?

Surah 8:48 Remember Satan made Their (sinful) acts seem Alluring to them, and said, "No one among men Can overcome you this day, While I am near you

Surah 14:22 And Satan will say When the matter is decided: "It was Allah Who gave you A promise of Truth: I too Promised, but I failed In my promise to you. I had no authority over you Except to call you, but ye Listened to me: then Reproach not me, but reproach Your own souls. I cannot listen To your cries, nor can ye Listen to mine. I reject Your

*former act in associating Me with Allah. For
wrongdoers there must be A Grievous Penalty.*

The Role or Activities of Jinn

According to Falzur Rahman, an Islamic scholar, Jinn are somewhere between an angel and a human. Other than their greater physical strength and fiery nature, they are not much different from human beings. Occasionally they materialize in different forms and can be seen by human eyes; however, they are normally invisible.

It is believed by most Muslims that Jinn can be converted; therefore, they have a soul making them human-like, which will spend eternity somewhere. Jinn were created that they might serve God.

*Surah 51:56 I have only created Jinns and men, that
They may serve Me.*

It is believed also by many Muslims that Jinn have had marriage relationships with humans, that they have even possessed humans, and that they perform mischief in the lives of humans.

The section of the Qur'an that was written in Medina does not contain any mention of the Jinn, while the sections written while in Mecca contains much about the Jinn. Muslim scholars of our day try to down play the Jinn and discussion of them.

The parts of the Qur'an written in Mecca report Jinn who listened to the prayers of Muslims, and the recitations of the Qur'an, were converted to Islam and faith in Allah.

Chapter XII
THE LAST DAYS AND SALVATION

Salvation According to Islam
Islam does not see man as fallen or in a state of depravity. Therefore, salvation is not to pick man up from some low estate. Islam does not see the need, as Christians do, for a Saviour to have died for their sins. This is because Islam believes that man has always been fundamentally good and that God loves and forgives those who obey his will.

Salvation in Islam is a future state experienced only after death and not at all in this life. Although they must become believers in this life, the benefits come in the life hereafter. Salvation is a pardon from all past sins, deliverance from hell, and acceptance into heaven.

Why Salvation Is Needed According To Islam
Salvation is needed because of man's weakness and forgetfulness that are inherent in his human nature. Islam does not see the need to be redeemed as Christians do. Islam does not use the term conversion, but rather uses the terms restoration, remembering, and returning with respect to salvation.

The word salvation only appears ten times in the Qur'an. Without salvation, they will spend eternity in the fire.

How Salvation Is Obtained According to Islam

Surah 23:102 Then those whose balance (of good

150

deeds) is heavy, --they will attain salvation:

This would imply that if their good works outweigh their bad works they can earn it.

> *Surah 3:191 Men who celebrate the praises of Allah, standing, sitting, and lying down on their sides, and contemplate the (wonders of) creation in the heavens and earth, (with the thought): "Our Lord! Not for naught hast Thou created (all) this! Glory to Thee! Give us Salvation from the penalty of the Fire.*

These positions that are mentioned are positions that they assume during their prayers.

> *Surah 85:11 For those who believe and do righteous deeds, will be Gardens beneath which Rivers flow: That is the great Salvation, (the fulfillment of all desires),*

Now, it is implied that they must believe or have faith, and work to attain salvation.

> *Surah 5:122 Allah will say: "This is a day on which the truthful will profit from their truth: Theirs are the Gardens, with rivers flowing beneath, --their eternal home": Allah well-pleased with them, and they with Allah: That is the great Salvation, (the fulfillment of desires).*

A new ingredient is now being added to the mixture for salvation. Truth is now required for salvation, but according to their own teaching, a Muslim is permitted or even encouraged to lie on four different occasion, especially when trying to deceive their enemies.

> *Surah 6:16 On that day, if the Penalty is averted*
> *from any, it is due to Allah's Mercy; and that would*
> *be (Salvation), the obvious fulfillment of all desire.*

Now, we have their salvation dependent upon the mercy of their god. According to what we saw earlier concerning the mercy of their god, I would not want to depend upon that.

> *Surah 9:20 Those who believe, and suffer exile and*
> *strive with might and main, in Allah's cause, with*
> *their goods and their persons, have the highest rank*
> *in the sight of Allah: They are the people who will*
> *achieve (salvation).*

Salvation has now become dependent upon a whole list of things. However, even if they have suffered and done all these things they still do not know if Allah has chosen them to be believers.

> *Surah 28:67 But any that (in this life) had repented,*
> *believed, and worked righteousness, will have hopes*
> *to be among those who achieve salvation.*

The word *"Hopes"* is plural, and in its plural form it has the meaning or implication that is to have no certainty/surety. It is saying that if I have done all these things, surely something will work, and I will have salvation.

As you can see in the verses from their own Qur'an, salvation is obtained by their good deeds and their belief in the oneness of Allah, and Muhammad as God's messenger, the prophecies of Muhammad, their belief in life after death, their belief in the resurrection, their belief in prayer, their belief in the angels, telling the truth, and being righteous. In addition, it depends on the fact of God's willingness to show them mercy.

If they are lacking in belief in any of these, then they are strictly at the mercy of Allah, and he may not have chosen them to be a true believer, and they may not attain salvation. After seeing the mercy of their God, I would not want to be dependent upon that mercy.

Assurance of Salvation According to Islam

Surah 39:61 But Allah will deliver the righteous to their place of salvation: No evil shall touch them, nor shall they grieve.

As you can see by the verse above, once they get there they have assurance, but prior to getting there, they have no real assurance. This is the only verse I could find in the entire Qur'an that could even be exaggerated to be alluding to assurance, and it really does not show assurance at all.

Many Muslim scholars have stated that no one can honestly say that they are a believer, for they do not know if Allah has chosen them to be one.

A noted Islamic scholar, Sufyan al-Thawri said, "He who says, 'I am a believer in the sight of God,' is a liar."

Others when asked, "Art thou a believer?" replied, "If it be the will of God."

To most Muslims the lack of assurance is not considered a weakness, but is simply a reality that motivates them to strive for obedience to Allah and the Qur'an.

Islam claims that there is no way that faith alone can constitute salvation or justification, but that God looks at the works and deeds to see who merits salvation. Yet, by their teaching, why would their God have to look at their works, for they cannot do good works unless Allah wills them to do it.

The Last Days According to Islam

Of course this is one of the five pillars of the faith of Islam so this is a very important issue. Their lack of belief in the Last Days would deny them salvation.

In many ways their beliefs in the Last Days is much like that of the Jews and Christians. However, they do have some very unique views dealing with the subject also.

Death According to Islam

Death is a certainty in the Qur'an as it is in the Bible. There is not much mentioned about the process of death in the Qur'an, but there are a few verses.

Surah 56:83 Then why do ye not (intervene) when (the soul of the dying man) reaches the throat,--

Surah 6:93 Who can be more wicked than one who inventeth a lie against Allah, or saith, "I have received inspiration," When he hath received none, or (again) who saith, "I can reveal the like of what Allah hath revealed"? If thou couldst but see how the wicked (do fare) in the flood of confusion at death! --The angels stretch forth their hands, (saying), "Yield up your souls: This day shall ye receive your reward, --a penalty of shame, for that ye used to tell lies against Allah, and scornfully to reject of His Signs!

154

Surah 8:50 If thou couldst see when the angels take the souls of the Unbelievers (at death), (how) they smite their faces and their backs, (saying): "Taste the Penalty of the blazing Fire—

Surah 79:1-2 By the (angels) who tear out (the souls of the wicked) with violence; By those who gently draw out (the souls of the blessed);

Surah 7:40 To those who reject Our Signs and treat them with arrogance, no opening will there be of the gates of heaven, nor will they enter the Garden, until the camel can pass through the eye of the needle: Such is Our reward for those in sin.

Beyond this the Qur'an does not say much concerning death, but Muslims then turn to the hadith for their teachings on death. They do not say a lot about the process of death, but they have teachings that go beyond death.

The Grave According to Islam

Surah 9:84 Nor do thou ever pray for any of them that dies, nor stand at his grave; for they rejected Allah and His Apostle, and died in a state of perverse rebellion.

Surah 80:21 Then He causeth him to die, and putteth him in his Grave;

These are the only two verses in the Qur'an where the word grave is used. All other information on the grave comes from the Hadith, which are the recorded deeds and sayings of Muhammad. Friends and followers of Muhammad recorded all his sayings and deeds contained in the Hadith after his death. The Hadith is second only to the Qur'an.

From the teachings in the Hadith, you will find what the majority of the Islam community believes concerning the grave.

Most Muslims believe that there are two angels that visit those in the grave and question them. It is not certain what all is asked of the dead, but there are three questions that are agreed upon by virtually all Muslims and most versions of the Hadith.

They are asked to sit up, and then are questioned.

1. Who is his Lord?
2. What is his religion?
3. Who is his prophet?

Only the true believers know the correct answers immediately, and they are: Allah, Islam, and Muhammad.

For the believers (those that answer correctly) their graves are made larger, (more spacious), and an open window is put in, through which they can view the Garden and receive the winds and odors of paradise.

On the other hand, for those that do not answer correctly there is a door opened to him. This door that is opened is to hell fire, and he feels the heat and hot winds from hell. Not only is the door opened, but also his grave is made smaller so that he is tormented and tortured in the grave for having not believed.

Some Muslims believe that everyone, even believers, will suffer some in the grave for things done while on earth. The Hadiths do not agree with each other concerning many things, but especially this subject. Some say that the dead cannot hear the living while others say they can. Some say that the punishment in the grave is only for a period of time while others say that there is punishment for the entire time in the grave. Some even say that the dead visit each other in the grave.

Concerning the dead, there is no one belief or theory that Islam as a whole accepts. As a matter of fact most of the modern Muslim writers do not even discuss the afterlife.

Heaven and Hell According to Islam

Heaven is mentioned forty-eight times in the Qur'an, and hell is mentioned eighty-two times. They are taught in the Qur'an as being real places where the souls of mankind will spend eternity. Heaven is the place that those to whom Allah chose to show mercy will be granted entrance, and hell is the place that those not chosen will be sent on the Day of Judgment.

The following is one description of hell from the Qur'an.

> *Surah 37: 62-68 Is that the better entertainment or the Tree of Zaqqum?*
> *63 For We have truly made it (as) a trial for the wrong-doers.*
> *64 For it is a tree that springs out of the bottom of Hell fire:*
> *65 The shoots of its fruit stalks are like the heads of devils:*
> *66 Truly they will eat thereof and fill their bellies therewith.*
> *67 Then on top of that they will be given a mixture made of boiling water.*
> *68 Then shall their return be to the (Blazing) Fire.*

The Qur'an says there will be water there. According to the Bible the temperature of hell is of such great degree that water would evaporate before it could even enter. The Bible says there was the plea in Luke 16:24 for one drop of water.

Luke 16:24 And he cried and said, Father Abraham, have mercy on me, and send Lazarus, that he may dip the tip of his finger in water, and cool my tongue; for I am tormented in this flame.

The following are verses using the word *Gardens* which refers to heaven. In the religion of Islam heaven and garden or gardens are synonymous.

"*Gardens*" is found seventy-five times in the Qur'an speaking of or referring to the home of the true believer.

Surah 18:31 For them will be Gardens of Eternity; beneath them rivers will flow: They will be adorned therein with bracelets of gold, and they will wear green garments of fine silk and heavy brocade; they will recline therein on raised thrones. How good the recompense! How beautiful a couch to recline on!

Surah 22:23 Allah will admit those who believe and work righteous deeds, to Gardens beneath which rivers flow: They shall be adorned therein with bracelets of gold and pearls; and their garments there will be of silk.

Surah 37:43 In Gardens of Felicity,

Felicity means anything that produces happiness and implies a place of peace or bliss.

Surah 55:54 They will recline on Carpets, whose inner linings will be of rich brocade: The Fruit of the Gardens will be near (and easy of reach).

One of the saddest things that I have seen as I have studied this religion is their view of heaven. Maybe I should say what makes heaven so great for them is so sad. If you will notice in the verses that I just gave, heaven's descriptions were gold, carpets, couches, thrones, silk, garments, and etc. There is not one mention that I have found anywhere in the Qur'an that mentions heaven being great because that is where God is and going there would mean getting to see Him or be with Him. To me heaven is heaven because of Jesus Christ the Lord, not anything else. The Muslim's heaven is based upon everything earthly and material. I will take my heaven over theirs any day.

Bodily Resurrection According to Islam

Surah 36:78-82 And he makes comparisons for Us, and forgets his own (origin and) Creation: He says, "Who can give life to (dry) bones and decomposed ones (at that)?"
79 Say, "He will give them life Who created them for the first time! For He is well-versed in every kind of creation! --
80 "The same Who produces for you fire out of the green tree, when behold! Ye kindle therewith (your own fires)!
81 "Is not He Who created the heavens and the earth able to create the like thereof?" --Yea, indeed! For He is the Creator Supreme, of skill and knowledge (infinite)!
82 Verily, when He intends a thing, His Command is, "Be", and it is!

Surah 46:33 See they not that Allah, Who created the heavens and the earth, and never wearied with their creation, is able to give life to the dead? Yea, verily He has power over all things.

Muhammad began his early preaching by proclaiming that there would be a bodily resurrection of all the dead. This caused many to mock him, but the Jews and the Christians basically taught the same thing.

Being Judged According to Islam

After all the dead are resurrected, they will be assembled before the throne of Allah. Some traditions say that all "will be barefoot, naked, and uncircumcised."

> *Surah 18:49 "And the Book (of Deeds) will be placed (before you); and thou wilt see the sinful in great terror because of what is (recorded) therein; they will say, "Ah! Woe to us! What a book is this! It leaves out nothing small or great, but takes account thereof! "They will find all that they did, placed before them: And not one will thy Lord treat with injustice."*

> *Surah 37:18-25 "Say thou: "Yea, and ye shall then be humiliated (on account of your evil)."*
> *19 Then it will be a single (compelling) cry; and behold, they will begin to see!*
> *20 They will say, "Ah! Woe to us! This is the Day of Judgment!"*
> *21 (A voice will say,) "This is the Day of Sorting Out, whose Truth ye (once) denied!"*
> *22 "Bring ye up", It shall be said, "the wrongdoers and their wives, and the things they worshipped--*
> *23 "Besides Allah, and lead them to the Way to the (Fierce) Fire!*
> *24 "But stop them, for they must be asked:*
> *25 "`What is the matter with you that ye help not*

each other?'''

Isn't it an injustice to this group of unbelievers if God did not choose them to believe? Is it not an injustice to punish the wives for the wrong doings of the husband? The verse asks them, "What is the matter with you that ye help not each other?" Therefore, the wife is being judged for the husband's wrong, but she is also being condemned for not helping the husband do right.

Surah 40:48 "Those who had been arrogant will say: "We are all in this (Fire)! Truly, Allah has judged between (His) Servants!"

Sentenced For All Eternity According to Islam

Surah 17:58 "There is not a population but We shall destroy it before the Day of Judgment or punish it with a dreadful Penalty: That is written in the (eternal) Record."

Surah 41:28 "Such is the requital of the enemies of Allah, --the Fire: Therein will be for them the Eternal Home: A (fit) requital, for that they were wont to reject Our Signs."

Surah 50:34 "Enter ye therein in Peace and Security; this is a Day of Eternal Life!"

Surah 17:13-19 "Every man's fate We have fastened on his own neck: On the Day of Judgment We shall bring out for him a scroll, which he will see spread open.
14 (It will be said to him:) "Read thine (own) record: Sufficient is thy soul this day to make out an account against thee."
15 Who receiveth guidance, receiveth it for his own

benefit: Who goeth astray doth so to his own loss: No bearer of burdens can bear the burden of another: Nor would We visit with Our Wrath until We had sent an apostle (to give warning).

16 When We decide to destroy a population, We (first) send a definite order to those among them who are given the good things of this life and yet transgress; so that the word is proved true against them: Then (it is) We destroy them utterly.

17 How many generations have We destroyed after Noah? And enough is thy Lord to note and see the sins of His servants.

18 If any do wish for the transitory things (of this life), We readily grant them--such things as We will, to such persons as We will: In the end have We provided Hell for them: They will burn therein, disgraced and rejected.

19 Those who do wish for the (things of) the Hereafter, and strive therefore with all due striving, and have Faith, --they are the ones whose striving is acceptable (to Allah)."

The last passage states, *"Every man's fate We have fastened on his own neck:"* and also says, *"No bearer of burdens can bear the burden of another."* What about the wives we just spoke of a moment ago? Their husband's fate was fastened on their necks, and they are definitely bearing the burdens of their husbands. They surely are not serving the same God that I serve in my Christian faith and walk. My God cannot judge unrighteously but will judge in truth and righteousness.

II Kings 14:6 But the children of the murderers he slew not: according unto that which is written in the book of the law of Moses, wherein the LORD commanded, saying, The fathers shall not be put to

162

death for the children, nor the children be put to death for the fathers; but every man shall be put to death for his own sin.

Surah 40:46 "In front of the Fire will they be brought, morning and evening: And (the Sentence will be) on the Day that Judgment will be established: "Cast ye the People of Pharaoh into the severest Penalty!"

Surah 50:24 "(The sentence will be:) "Throw, throw into Hell every contumacious Rejecter (of Allah)!--"

Islam does teach and believe that the sentence is eternal in either heaven or hell. The eternal salvation or eternal damnation is a central theme that runs through the Qur'an and is used to prompt those of Islam to serve Allah whole-heartedly.

Because of Islam's belief about the Last Days, they stand strong on the judgment that Allah will pass and that it will be eternal.

The word eternity appears eleven times in the Qur'an, and all but one refers to eternity in the Gardens. Only one refers to eternity in hell because of evil deeds.

Chapter XIII
ISLAM'S VIEW OF CREATION

Islam does acknowledge God as the creator of all that is and ever will be. However, their view is quite different from that of Jewish or Christian beliefs. We will look at just a few of their beliefs.

Six Days of Creation

Surah 7:54 Your Guardian-Lord is Allah, Who created the heavens and the earth in six Days, and is firmly established on the Throne (of authority): He draweth the night as a veil Over the day, each seeking the other in rapid succession: He created the sun, the moon, and the stars, (all) governed by laws under His Command. Is it not His to create and to govern? Blessed be Allah, the Cherisher and Sustainer of the Worlds!

Surah 10:3 Verily your Lord is Allah, Who created the heavens and the earth in six Days, and is firmly established on the Throne (of authority), regulating and governing all things. No intercessor (can plead with Him) except after His leave (hath been obtained). This is Allah your Lord; Him therefore serve Will ye not receive admonition?

The previous verses attack Christ as the intercessor for you and me, and it is so out of place. It does not fit in the passage at all, but the devil hates Christ so much that he takes every

164

opportunity he can to try to discredit Him.

> *Surah 11:7 He it is Who created the heavens and the earth in six Days--and His Throne was over the Waters--that He might try you, which of you is best in conduct. But if thou wert to say to them "Ye shall indeed be raised up after death", the Unbelievers would be sure to say, "This is nothing but obvious sorcery!"*

> *Surah 25:59 He Who created the heavens and the earth and all that is between, in six days, and is firmly established on the Throne (of authority): Allah Most Gracious: Ask thou, then, about Him of any acquainted (with such things).*

> *Surah 32:4 It is Allah Who has created the heavens and the earth, and all between them, in six Days, and is firmly established on the Throne (of authority): Ye have none, besides Him, to protect or intercede (for you): Will ye not then receive admonition?*

These verses again make an attack upon Christ as the one who intercedes for you and me, and it is so out of place. It does not flow in the passage at all, but as we said earlier, the devil hates Christ so much that he takes every opportunity he can to try to discredit Him.

> *Surah 50:38 "We created the heavens and the earth and all between them in Six Days, nor did any sense of weariness touch Us."*

> *Surah 57:4 He it is Who created the heavens and the earth in six Days, and is moreover firmly*

established on the Throne (of authority). He knows what enters within the earth and what comes forth out of it, what comes down from heaven and what mounts up to it. And He is with you wheresoever ye may be. And Allah sees well all that ye do.

Two Days of Creation

Surah 41:9 Say: "Is it that ye deny Him Who created the earth in two Days? And do ye join equals with Him? He is the Lord of (all) the Worlds.

Surah 41:12 So he completed them as seven firmaments in two Days, and He assigned to each heaven its duty and command. And We adorned the lower heaven with lights, and (provided it) with guard. Such is the Decree of (Him) the Exalted in Might, Full of Knowledge.

After all the verses that we saw earlier stating six days, now we have two verses that are declaring the Creation in two days. So that we can get the whole picture now, we will give you the complete passage with verses 10-11 included. This way we cannot be accused of pulling the verses out of context which is a general practice of most Muslims when they use the Bible.

The Creation of Heaven and Earth According to Islam

Surah 41:9-12 Say: "Is it that ye deny Him Who created the earth in two Days? And do ye join equals with Him? He is the Lord of (all) the Worlds. 10 He set on the (earth) mountains standing firm, high above it, and bestowed blessings on the earth, and measured therein all things to give them nourishment in due proportion, in four Days, in

166

accordance with (the needs of) those who seek (sustenance).
11 Moreover He comprehended in His design the sky, and it had been (as) smoke: He said to it and to the earth: "Come ye together, willingly or unwillingly." They said: "We do come (together), in willing obedience."
12 So he completed them as seven firmaments in two Days, and He assigned to each heaven its duty and command. And We adorned the lower heaven with lights, and (provided it) with guard. Such is the Decree of (Him) the Exalted in Might, Full of Knowledge.

This passage creates some major problems for the Muslim. After all the passages that said very plainly that creation took place in six days, now we have if you add it all up in this passage eight days. This is one of those times that the Muslim will say we should look at the notes.

The note pertaining to the statement: "The earth in two Days?" for verse 9 is note 4470, and I love what it says.

Note 4470 – "This is a difficult passage, describing the primal Creation of our physical earth and the physical heavens around us. If we count the two days mentioned in this verse, the four days, mentioned in verse 10, and the two days mentioned in verse 12, we get a total of eight days. While in many other passages the creation is stated to have taken place in six days:" The translator then lists several of the verses referred to earlier referencing to a six-day Creation. Then he tries to explain it like this, "The Commentators understand the "four days" in verse 10 to include the two days in verse 9, so that the total for the universe comes to six days. This is reasonable because the processes described in verses 9 and 10 form really one series. In the one case it is the

Creation of the formless matter of the earth; and in the other case it is the gradual evolution of the earth, its mountains and seas, and its animal and vegetable life, with the "nourishment in due proportion," proper to each."

Now they have brought evolution into the picture trying to explain away their lack of understanding. When most Muslims see this, they really do not know what to say, but many will still try to argue the point.

Now in verse 41:12 when it says "In two days," which is the second time two days appeared in this passage. It gives another note to refer to.

Note 4470 – "For 'days', which may include thousands of years, they refer to stages in the evolution of physical nature. In the Biblical cosmogony, (Gen. I, and II. 1-7), which reflects old Babylonian cosmogony, the scheme is apparently to be taken literally as two days and is as follows: (Here the translator lists the Bible account for each day of Creation in his notes then follows with) Our scheme is wholly different. (1) Allah did not rest and never rests... (2) Allah's work has not ended; his activity still goes on... (3) Man in our scheme does not come in with the land animals; his advent is much later. (4) Our stages are not sharply divided from each other, as in the above scheme...."

The translator then tries to explain his scheme in the remainder of the note 4470 – "Our six stages are broadly speaking, (1) the throwing off of our planet from cosmic matter; (2) its cooling and condensing, (3) and (4) the growth of vegetable and animal life; (5) and (6) the parallel growth of the starry realm and our solar system."

I can tell you from experience that many of the Muslims with whom I have had opportunity to share these things have been totally shocked, because they have never read it. They have just accepted that the Qur'an taught the six days of Creation like they had always heard. Now they are hit with the Qur'an translator teaching evolution. The Big Bang Theory implies evolution and not theistic evolution. I added theistic evolution into the equation because the translator and the Qur'an repeatedly say created, but then the translator keeps throwing evolution into the formula in his notes. He speaks of a throwing off of cosmic matter (Big Bang) but then tries to explain creation.

In the previous passage we see two days and four days and two days all being attributed to the length of time in which God created the heavens and the earth. So needless to say there is a great controversy for them to reason out now. We have cast much doubt upon their teachings.

Islam claims that because of the order that exists in creation, it shows God's oneness, but it also shows that it is subject to God's law. Therefore, Islam claims that even the earth is Islamic because it has submitted to God.

Creation of Angelic Beings According to Islam

Archangels
There are four Archangels that were mentioned as being created for special tasks. Those were Gabriel, Michael, Israfil, and Izra'il.

Angels
This group of angels, as we discussed earlier, were given specific jobs such as recording, guarding, receiving, and errands.

Jinn
Surah 51:56 "I have only created Jinns and men, that they may serve Me."

Interesting Note: A RACE CAN REPRODUCE

Surah 15:27 "And the Jinn race, We had created before, from the fire of a scorching wind."

The Qur'an devotes the whole surah 72 to the Jinn, but as we saw the Jinn are very different in that they are half human and half angel. They seem to meddle in the lives of humans in many ways and seem to be very curious of human activities.

Satan

Reason for Satan's Fall
As we saw earlier in the course, Satan's refusal to bow down before Adam when God commanded the angels to prostrate themselves before his Creation was when God cast him out of Heaven, which is also called the garden.

Satan's mission After His Fall
Satan's mission after his fall was to deceive mankind and try to keep them from entering heaven.

Surah 7:11-18 "It is We Who created you and gave you shape; then We bade the angels bow down to Adam, and they bowed down; not so Iblis; he refused to be of those who bow down.
12 (Allah) said: "What prevented thee from bowing down when I commanded thee?" He said: "I am better than he: Thou didst create me from fire,"
13 (Allah) said: "Get thee down from this: It is not for thee to be arrogant here: Get out, for thou art of the meanest (of creatures)."
14 He said: "Give me respite till the day they are raised up."

15 (Allah) said: "Be thou among those who have respite."
16 He said: "Because thou hast thrown me out of the Way, lo! I will lie in wait for them on Thy Straight Way:"
17 "Then will I assault them from before them and behind them, from their right and their left: Nor wilt Thou find, in most of them gratitude (for Thy mercies)."
18 (Allah) said: "Get out from this, disgraced and expelled. If any of them follow thee, --Hell will I fill with you all."

Surah 7:61-64 Behold! We said to the angels: "Bow down unto Adam": They bowed down except Iblis: He said, "Shall I bow down to one whom Thou didst create from clay?"
62 He said, "Seest Thou? This is the one whom Thou hast honored above me! If Thou wilt but respite me to the Day of Judgment, I will surely bring his descendants under my sway--all but a few!"
63 (Allah) said: "Go thy way; if any of them follow thee, verily Hell will be the recompense of you (all) --an ample recompense.
64 "Lead to destruction those whom thou canst among them, with thy (seductive) voice; make assaults on them with thy cavalry and thy infantry; mutually share with them wealth and children; and make promises to them." But Satan promises them nothing but deceit.

In this last passage the Qur'an says God told Satan to go and try to deceive them if he could. How can Satan deceive them unless God wills them to be deceived?

171

Creation of Human Beings

Surah 15:26 "We created man from sounding clay, from mud molded into shape;"

The Qur'an does say that Adam was the first man that God created. However there is controversy concerning where he was created. Most Muslims say he was created in Heaven and that he was kicked out after he sinned.

> *Surah 32:9 But He fashioned him In due proportion, and breathed Into him something of His spirit. And He gave You (the faculties of) hearing And sight and feeling (and understanding): Little thanks do ye give!*

> *Surah 21:91 And (remember) her who guarded her chastity: We breathed into her of Our Spirit, and We made her and her son a Sign for all peoples.*

I would like to draw your attention to something. In surah 21:91 when speaking of "Christ" as "Spirit" capital "S" is used. Surah 32:9 speaks of Adam using a small "s" noting the deity of Christ even in their Qur'an by the capitalization of the word Spirit. This is another ray of light that God has commanded to shine forth.

> *Surah 2:30 Behold, thy Lord said to the angels: "I will create A vicegerent of earth." They said: "Wilt Thou place therein one who will make Mischief therein and shed blood?--Whilst we do celebrate Thy praised And glorify Thy holy (name)?" He said: "I know what ye know not."*

Angels cannot sin according to Islam, but here we have the

Angels questioning God?

Here we must question, are the angels omniscient? The reason I say this is because the question they ask tells that they knew what man would do.

Vicegerent: (vis' jir' ent), A person appointed by another to exercise the latter's power and authority; a deputy.

The Qur'an does not tell of Eve's creation but following God's announcement of creating Adam in surah 2:30, we find in surah 2:35 Eve is now present with Adam in front of the angels. In addition, by what the following passage says they must have been created in Heaven for they are in the garden and are being told to dwell in the garden. We will see more evidence of their position later.

> *Surah 2:35a "We said, O Adam! dwell thou And thy wife in the Garden; And eat of the bountiful things therein"*
>
> *Surah 2:31-34 And He taught Adam the names Of all things; then He placed them Before the angels, and said: "Tell Me The names of these if ye are right."*
> *32 They said: "Glory to Thee: of knowledge We have none, save what Thou Hast taught us: in truth it is Thou Who art perfect in knowledge and wisdom."*
> *33 He said: O Adam! tell them Their names." When he had told them, Allah said: "Did I not tell you That I know the secrets of heaven And the earth, and I know what ye reveal And what ye conceal?"*
> *34 And behold, We said to the angels: Bow down to Adam:" and they bowed down: Not so Iblis: he*

*refused and was haughty: He was of those who
reject Faith.*

According to this passage in the Qur'an, man is given authority over the angels and Satan's refusal to bow down to man was where his pride showed up. This is quite the opposite from the Bible account of the creation of man. This passage also says, "He placed them before the angels," Who is being referred to as *them*? Since most Islamic scholars believe that Eve's creation, even though there is no account given in the Qur'an of it, was after the angels had bowed down to Adam. "Them" is plural and points to the fact of Eve being with Adam at the time they were brought before the angels.

This passage also denotes man's superiority to angels in their capacity for learning, growth, and importance. God declared that the angels were commanded to bow down to man.

This passage has also caused much controversy among the Muslims because of their rigid stand that only God (Allah) deserves to be worshipped, and here we have God (Allah) ordering the angels to worship (bow down to) man.

In the following passage we see that soon after the creation of Adam and Eve in the Garden, Satan began to deceive them. Satan was angry with them because it was Satan's refusal to bow down to Adam that caused God to cast him out of heaven. Satan accomplished what he set out to do and deceived Adam and Eve, and they were eventually expelled from heaven also.

The Qur'an seems to imply that the Garden was in Heaven and that the two places are one and the same as we have already stated.

*Surah 7:20-25 Then began Satan to whisper
suggestions to them, In order to reveal to them*

*Their shame That was hidden from them (Before):
he said: "Your Lord Only forbade you this tree, Lest
ye should become angels Or such beings as live
forever."
21 And he swore to them Both, that he was Their
sincere adviser.
22 So by deceit he brought about Their fall: (the
Fall of Man) when they Tasted of the tree, Their
shame became manifest To them, and they began To
sew together the leaves Of the Garden over their
bodies. And their Lord called Unto them: "Did I not
Forbid you that tree, And tell you that Satan Was an
avowed Enemy unto you?"
23 They said: Our Lord! We have wronged our
own souls: If Thou forgive us not And bestow not
upon us Thy Mercy, we shall Certainly be lost."
24 (Allah) said: "Get ye down, With enmity
between yourselves. On earth will be your
dwelling -place And your means of livelihood--For
a time.
25 He said: "Therein shall ye Live, and therein
shall ye Die; but from it shall ye Be taken out (at
last)."*

The passage said, *"So by deceit he brought about Their fall."* Note the direction of their fall, *"Get ye down, With enmity between yourselves. On earth will be your dwelling place And your means of livelihood--For a time. He said: "Therein shall ye Live, and therein shall ye Die; but from it shall ye Be taken out (at last)."*

Did you notice that it said with enmity between yourselves? If you remember earlier, there were husbands and wives being cast into hell, and they were asked why they did not help each other. The following is that passage; notice what it says.

Surah 37:18-25 Say thou: "Yea, and ye shall then be humiliated (on account of your evil)."
19 Then it will be a single (compelling) cry; and behold, they will begin to see!
20 They will say, "Ah! Woe to us! This is the Day of Judgment!"
21 (A voice will say,) "This is the Day of Sorting Out, whose truth ye (once) denied!"
22 "Bring ye up", it shall be said, "The wrong-doers and their wives, and the things they worshipped-
23 "Besides Allah, and lead them to the Way to the (Fierce) Fire!
24 "But stop them, for they must be asked:
25 "'What is the matter with you that ye help not each other?'"

The problem with the family in this passage is the enmity that God put between Adam and Eve when they were cast down to earth.

Another account of the Fall of Adam is in Surah 2:34-39.

Surah 2:34-39 And behold, We said to the angels: "Bow down to Adam:" And they bowed down: Not so Iblis: He refused and was haughty: He was of those who reject Faith.
35 We said: "O Adam! Dwell thou and thy wife in the Garden; and eat of the bountiful things therein as (where and when) ye will; but approach not this tree, or ye run into harm and transgression."
36 Then did Satan make them slip from the (Garden), and get them out of the state (of felicity) in which they had been. We said: "Get ye down, all (ye people) with enmity between yourselves. On earth will be your dwelling place and your means of

livelihood—for a time."
37 Then learnt Adam from his Lord words of inspiration, and his Lord turned towards him, for He is Oft-Returning, Most Merciful.
38 We said: "Get ye down all from here; and if, as is sure, there comes to you guidance from Me, whosoever follows My guidance, on them shall be no fear, nor shall they grieve."
39 "But those who reject Faith and belie Our Signs, they shall be Companions of the Fire; they shall abide therein."

Notice in verse 36 it is referred to as a slip and not a fall.

That is a mighty big slip from Heaven to earth; I think it would be better described as the fall of man.

Why then, since in Surah 2:31-34, angels bowed down to man, does Satan tempt Adam and Eve to eat of the tree so they can become angels or beings that would live eternally when they were sinless and would live that way already? Why would they even listen to Satan when they were present when Satan requested permission to deceive them?

This passage also notes that Satan deceived both of them, and not as our account is given in the Bible that Eve was deceived and took of the fruit of the tree and then gave it to Adam.

Surah 2:31-34 tell us that Adam was the one with wisdom and not the angels. Adam told the names of all things to the angels which demonstrated his knowledge being greater than the angels. Yet in surah 7:20-25 when Satan tempts or deceives Adam and Eve: "And he swore to them Both, that he was Their sincere advisor." Why would they believe one they knew had less wisdom than they had?

177

The anti-Christ will also attempt to deceive in the same fashion during the first half of the tribulation. He will swear to the Jews to be their friend and promise peace, but after three and one half years, he will reveal to the world his true identity. Just like Christ ministered for three and one half years and demonstrated to the world He was indeed the Savior when He laid down His life for you and me.

According to Biblical Christianity, as a result of the Fall, Adam and Eve were cast out of the garden, and as a result of Adam's sin, all mankind has the sin nature. Muslims believe that Adam and Eve's eating of the tree was only a single slip and when they repented God (Allah) forgave them, and it had no further effect on the nature of man or any on creation. They also explain that the command God gave "get ye down" was made after God had forgiven or pardoned them. They believed that Adam left Heaven and had to come to earth as God's vicegerent or viceroy (deputy sovereign; representative ruler). In other words Adam had to come down to earth to manage it.

Islam teaches that we are born innocent and remain innocent until we commit a guilty act or deed, and if we repent we are totally forgiven. Because we are born innocent and are not fallen, we have no need of a Savior. However, Muslims are not saved and do not claim to be either; they need to do good works and to do them ethically so they will go to Heaven.

I dealt with a Muslim inmate in Kentucky State Prison who believed the things we just stated. He said that, "Adam's slip or sin has had no effect upon any of us." So I asked if he had been to Heaven yet or knew anyone that had been to Heaven. He told me that he did not know of anyone but that he hoped to go someday. I asked him then, "If Adam's sin has had no effect upon us, why do we have to start where he fell in hopes of getting to go to where he started?" Of course he had not looked at it like that, and so I said, "It looks to me like Adam's sin has impacted everyone that has ever been born. For we have to start out in a fallen state hoping to go to Heaven one day. Adam's slip sure sounds like a fall that has affected every one of us." He was totally shocked when he saw that the Qur'an actually said, "So by deceit he brought about their fall when they tasted of the tree."

> *Romans 5:12 Wherefore, as by one man sin entered into the world, and death by sin; and so death passed upon all men, for that all have sinned:*

The following verses from the Qur'an explain man's creation. Notice all the different things from which man is made according to the Qur'an, even things that are dead, like clots of blood and congealed blood. Notice also how they contradict each other, and there is no consistency.

> *Surah 22:36b ... "We made animals subject to you, that ye May be grateful"*

> *Surah 16:4 He has created man from a sperm drop; and behold this same (man) becomes an open disputer!*

> *Surah 18:37 His companion said to him, in the course of the argument with him: "Dost thou deny Him Who created thee out of dust, then out of a sperm drop, then fashioned thee into a man?*

> *Surah 22:5 "O mankind! If ye have a doubt about the Resurrection, (consider) that We created you out of dust, then out of sperm, then out of a leech like clot; then out of a morsel of flesh, partly formed and partly unformed, in order that We may manifest*

(Our Power) to you; and We cause whom We will to rest in the wombs for an appointed term, then do We bring you out as babes, then (foster you) that ye may reach your age of full strength; and some of you are called to die, and some are sent back to the feeblest old age, so that they know nothing after having known (much). And (further), thou seest the earth barren and lifeless, but when We pour down rain on it, it is stirred (to life), it swells, and it puts forth every kind of beautiful growth (in pairs)."

Surah 23:13 "Then We placed him as (a drop of) sperm in a place of rest, firmly fixed;"

Surah 23:14 "Then We made the sperm into a clot of congealed blood; then of that clot We made a (foetus) lump; then We made out of that lump bones and clothed the bones with flesh; then We developed out of it another creature. So blessed be Allah, the Best to create!"

Surah 35:11 And Allah did create you from dust; then from a sperm-drop. Then He made you in pairs. And no female conceives, or lays down (her load), but with His knowledge. Nor is a man long-lived granted length of days, nor is a part cut off from his life, but is in a Decree (ordained). All this is easy to Allah.

Surah 36:77 "Doth not man see that it is We Who created him from sperm? Yet behold! He (stands forth) as an open adversary!"

Surah 40:67 It is He Who has created you from dust, then from a sperm drop, then from a leech like clot; then does He get you out (into the light) as a child: Then lets you (grow and) reach your age of full strength; then lets you become old, --though of you there are some who die before; --and lets you reach a Term appointed; in order that ye may learn wisdom.

Surah 75:37 Was he not a drop of sperm emitted (in lowly form)?

Surah 76:2 "Verily We created Man from a drop of mingled sperm, in order to try him: So We gave him (the gifts) of Hearing and Sight."

Surah 80:19 From a sperm drop: He hath created him, and then moulded him in due proportions;

Surah 25:54 It is He Who has created man from water: Then has He established relationships of lineage and marriage: For thy Lord has power (over all things).

Surah 95:4 "We have indeed created man in the best of moulds,"

Surah 96:2 Created man, out of a (mere) clot of congealed blood:

Surah 49:13 "O mankind! We created You from a single (pair) Of a male and a female, And made you into Nations and tribes, that Ye may know each other (Not that ye may despise each other)."

Surah 7:24 "Say with enmity between yourselves) Verily the most honoured of you In the sight of

181

Allah Is (he who is) the most Righteous of you. And Allah has full knowledge And is well-acquainted (with all things)."

Surah 7:24 "Says with enmity between yourselves."

The general consensus or view of Islam is that man is not to attempt to know God or conform to God's character, but man is to understand God's will and become more obedient to God's commands. The Qur'an's emphasis is not on revealing who God is, but on what God wills as man's highest calling.

The Garden of Islam
It is believed by most in Islam that the garden was in Heaven. The reason for this is found in Surah 7:20-25 when Satan deceives Adam and Eve, God then tells Adam and Eve to "Get ye down." Down meant from Heaven to the earth; the same passage states that earth would be their home until they died and God would bring them back to heaven in reference to the resurrection.

Also, as we saw earlier in the study, the word *gardens* referred to the final abode of the true believer.

Chapter XIV
KORAN (QUR'AN) REFERENCES TO USE

To Show That Jesus Performed Miracles

The following verses tell of some of the miracles that Jesus performed while on earth. Note that the doing of miracles was a requirement for being a prophet. In a little while we will see that Muhammad did no miracles. This makes it hard to understand how Islam can recognize Muhammad as a greater prophet than Jesus, who did many miracles and entered the world through a miraculous conception.

Notice in the following verses from the Qur'an that "Trinity" is very plain in the statement, "I strengthened thee with the Holy Spirit." God is the *I*, Jesus is the *thee*, and the Holy Spirit.

Surah 5:110-115 Then will Allah say: "O Jesus the son of Mary! Recount My favor to thee and to thy mother Behold! I strengthened thee with the holy spirit, so that thou didst speak to the people in childhood and in maturity. Behold! I taught thee the Book and Wisdom, and behold! Thou makest out of clay, as it were, the figure of a bird, by My leave, and thou breathest into it, and it becometh a bird by My leave, and thou healest those born blind, and the lepers, by My leave. And behold! Thou bringest forth the dead by My leave. And behold! I did restrain the Children of Israel from (violence to) thee when thou didst show them the Clear Signs, and the unbelievers among them said: 'This is nothing but evident magic'."

183

111 "And behold! I inspired the Disciples to have faith in Me and Mine Apostle: They said: 'We have faith, and do thou bear witness that we bow to Allah as Muslims'."
112 Behold! The Disciples said: "O Jesus the son of Mary! Can thy Lord send down to us a Table set (with viands) from heaven?" Said Jesus: "Fear Allah, if ye have faith."
113 They said: "We only wish to eat thereof and satisfy our hearts, and to know that thou hast indeed told us the truth; and that we ourselves may be witnesses to the miracle."
114 Said Jesus the son of Mary: "O Allah our Lord! Send us from heaven a Table set (with viands), that there may be for us--for the first and last of us--a solemn festival and a Sign from Thee; and provide for our sustenance, for Thou art the best Sustainer (of our needs)."
115 Allah said: "I will send it down unto you: But if any of you after that resisteth faith, I will punish him with a penalty such as I have not inflicted on any one among all the peoples."

The following passages tell of the virgin birth of Jesus.

Surah 19:16-22 Relate in the Book (the story of) Mary, when she withdrew from her family to a place in the East.
17 She placed a screen (to screen herself) from them; then We sent to her Our angel, and he appeared before her as a man in all respects.
18 She said: "I seek refuge from thee to (Allah) Most Gracious: (Come not near) if thou dost fear Allah."
19 He said: "Nay, I am only a messenger from

184

thy Lord, (to announce) to thee the gift of a holy son."
20 She said: "How shall I have a son, seeing that no man has touched me, and I am not Unchaste?"
21 He said: "So (it will be): Thy Lord saith, 'That is easy for Me: And (We wish) to appoint him as a Sign unto men and a Mercy from Us': It is a matter (so) decreed."
22 So she conceived him and she retired with him to a remote place.

Surah 19:27-34 At length she brought the (babe) to her people, carrying him (in her arms). They said: "O Mary! Truly an amazing thing hast thou brought!
28 "O sister of Aaron! Thy father was not a man of evil, nor thy mother a woman unchaste!"
29 But she pointed to the babe. They said: "How can we talk to one who is a child in the cradle?"
30 He said: "I am indeed a servant of Allah: He hath given me revelation and made me a prophet;
31 "And He hath made me blessed wheresoever I be, and hath enjoined on me Prayer and Charity as long as I live;
32 "(He) hath made me kind to my mother, and not overbearing or miserable;
33 "So Peace is on me the day I was born, the day that I die, and the day that I shall be raised up to life (again)"!
34 Such (was) Jesus the son of Mary: (It is) a statement of truth, about which they (vainly) dispute.

The previous passage foretells Jesus' birth, death, and resurrection. Still yet those of Islam deny the crucifixion of Jesus and that He actually died.

> *Surah 4:157-159 That they said (in boast), "We killed Christ Jesus the son of Mary, the Apostle of Allah"; --But they killed him not, nor crucified him, but so it was made to appear to them, and those who differ therein are full of doubts, with no (certain) knowledge, but only conjecture to follow, for of a surety they killed him not: --*
> *158 Nay, Allah raised him up unto Himself; and Allah is Exalted in Power, Wise; --*
> *159 And there is none of the People of the Book but must believe in him before his death; and on the Day of Judgment he will be a witness against them;--"*

To Show That Moses And Prophets Of God Performed Miracles

> *Surah 7:106-108 (Pharaoh) said: "If indeed thou hast come with a Sign, show it forth, --if thou tellest truth."*
> *107 Then (Moses) threw his rod, and behold! It was a serpent, plain (for all to see)!*
> *108 And he drew out his hand, and behold! It was white to all beholders!*

> *Surah 7:116-119 Said Moses: "Throw ye (first)." So when they threw, they bewitched the eyes of the people, and struck terror into them: For they showed a great (feat of) magic.*
> *117 We put it into Moses's mind By inspiration:*

186

"Throw (now) thy rod": And behold! It swallows up straightway all the falsehoods which they fake!
118 Thus truth was confirmed. And all that they did was made of no effect.
119 So the (great ones) were vanquished there and then, and were made to look small.

Surah 23:45 "Then We sent Moses and his brother Aaron, with Our Signs and Authority manifest,"

Surah 4:153 The People of the Book ask thee to cause a book to descend to them from heaven: Indeed they asked Moses for an even greater (miracle), for they said: "Show us Allah in public," But they were dazed for their presumption, with thunder and lightning. Yet they worshipped the calf even after Clear Signs had come to them; even so We forgave them; and gave Moses manifest proofs of authority."

Moses, according to Islam, has proof that he qualifies to be a prophet by doing miracles.

To Show That Muhammad Never Performed Any Miracles

Surah 17:90-94 They say: "We shall not believe in thee, until thou cause a spring to gush forth for us from the earth,
91 "Or (until) thou have a garden of date trees and vines, and cause rivers to gush forth in their midst, carrying abundant water;
92 "Or thou cause the sky to fall in pieces, as

*thou sayest (will happen), against us; or thou
bring Allah and the angels before (us) face to
face;*
*93 "Or thou have a house adorned with gold, or
thou mount a ladder right into the skies. No, we
shall not even believe in thy mounting until thou
send down to us a book that we could read."
Say: "Glory to my Lord! Am I aught but a man,
--an apostle?"*
*94 What kept men back from Belief when
Guidance came to them, was nothing but this:
They said, "Has Allah sent a man (like us) to be
(His) Apostle?"*

Islam is constantly saying that Muhammad did many miracles.
However, there are none found in the Qur'an to support their
claim. Their entire basis for any purported miracles comes from
traditions and other writings, but nothing is found in their most
holy book the Qur'an. The Qur'an does record assumed miracles
that their other prophets performed which confirms that they were
indeed prophets.

Even Abdullah Yusuf Ali (the translator of the Qur'an),
admitted that Muhammad did not perform any miracles. This
raised many questions and doubts concerning Muhammad's
credentials as a prophet.

*Surah 6:37 They say: "Why is not a Sign sent
down to him from his Lord?" Say: "Allah hath
certainly power to send down a Sign: But most
of them understand not."*

*Surah 10:20 They say: "Why is not a Sign sent
down to him from his Lord?" Say: "The Unseen
is only for Allah (to know). then wait ye: I too*

will wait with you. "

Surah 6:8 They say: "Why is not an angel sent down to him?" If We did send down an angel, the matter would be settled at once, and no respite would be granted them. "

Surah 4:153 The People of the Book ask thee to cause a book to descend to them from heaven: Indeed they asked Moses for an even greater (miracle), for they said: "Show us Allah in public," But they were dazed for their presumption, with thunder and lightning. Yet they worshipped the calf even after Clear Signs had come to them; even so We forgave them; and gave Moses manifest proofs of authority.

Even with all the challenges to perform a miracle by the people, Muhammad never did. Moses did when he was challenged; Jesus did when he was challenged but not Muhammad.

To Show Islam's Grounds for Religious Wars or Fighting

Surah 2:244-245 Then fight in the cause of Allah, and know that Allah heareth and knoweth all things.
245 Who is he that will loan to Allah a beautiful loan, which Allah will double unto his credit and multiply many times? It is Allah that giveth (you) Want or Plenty, and to Him shall be your return.

Surah 9:5 But when the forbidden months are past, then fight and slay the Pagans wherever ye find them, and seize them, beleaguer them, and

189

*lie in wait for them in every stratagem (of war);
but if they repent, and establish regular prayers
and practice regular charity, then open the way
for them: For Allah is Oft-Forgiving, Most
Merciful.*

Surah 9:5 said slay the Pagans (all non-Muslims) wherever
you find them. It also says, "But if they repent," but how can they
repent when they have been slain. Islam is not interested in
subduing Jews and Christians; they are out to destroy them. They
are told to do so in their Qur'an. Those that say otherwise are
lying; they believe lying is permissible to deceive their enemies.
The media is publishing a false image of Islam. Islam is not
peaceful, loving, and tolerant of other religions; society is
swallowing it up. Muslims hate us and are set to destroy all non-
Muslims.

*Surah 47:4 Therefore, when ye meet the
Unbelievers (in fight), smite at their necks; at
length, when ye have thoroughly subdued them,
bind a bond firmly (on them): Thereafter (is the
time for) either generosity or ransom: Until the
war lays down its burdens. Thus (are ye
commanded): But if it had been Allah's Will, He
could certainly have exacted retribution from
them (Himself); but (He lets you fight) in order
to test you, some with others. But those who are
slain in the way of Allah, --He will never let
their deeds be lost.*

The previous verse said to smite at their necks, which is a
deathblow. It is not a blow to subdue an enemy, but it is to destroy
with certainty. The statement totally contradicts the rest of the
verse. There is no way to show generosity afterward or ransom.

> *Surah 9:29 Fight those who believe not in Allah nor the Last Day, nor hold that forbidden which hath been forbidden by Allah and His Apostle, nor acknowledge the Religion of Truth, (even if they are) of the People of the Book, until they pay the Jizya with willing submission, and feel themselves subdued.*

Earlier they were not to fight the People of the Book, but now the attitude towards Jews and Christians has changed.

> *Surah 4:95 Not equal are those Believers who sit (at home) and receive no hurt, and those who strive and fight in the cause of Allah with their goods and their persons. Allah hath granted a grade higher to those who strive and fight with their goods and persons than to those who sit (at home). Unto all (in Faith) hath Allah promised good: But those who strive and fight hath He distinguished above those who sit (at home) by a special reward,--*

The previous verse gives encouragement to be of those that give their all (suicide bombers?) and not to be like those that sit at home uninvolved. This is why many Muslims give their all (to the point of being a suicide bomber) so that they will be pleasing in Allah's sight.

> *Surah 3:85 If anyone desires A religion other than Islam (submission to Allah), Never will it be accepted Of him; and in the Heareafter He will be in the ranks Of those who have lost (All spiritual good).*

As you can plainly see from the above verse the religion o

Islam is not at all tolerant of other religions. The media would have you to think they are peaceable, but actually, they are not.

> *Surah 5:54 O ye who believe! If any from among you Turnback from his Faith, Soon will Allah produce A people whom He will love As they will love Him -- Lowly with the Believers, Mighty against the Rejecters, Fighting in the Way of Allah, And never afraid Of the reproaches Of such as find fault. That is the Grace of Allah, Which He will bestow On whom He pleaseth. And Allah encompasseth all, And He knoweth all things.*

I think it is clear to see why many Muslims are militant in their actions and their reasoning.

Muhammad's change in attitude towards Christians
In Muhammad's first writings in the Qur'an, in Mecca and early Medina, he encouraged and demonstrated a friendly attitude towards both Jews and Christians.

> *Surah 2:62 Those who believe (in the Qur'an) And those who follow the Jewish (scriptures), And the Christians and the Sabians -- Any who believe in Allah And the Last Day, And work righteousness, Shall have their reward With their Lord; in them Shall be no fear, nor shall they grieve.*

> *Surah 29:46 And dispute ye not With the People of the Book, Except with means better (Than mere disputation), unless It Be with those of them Who inflict wrong (and injury); But say, "We believe In the Revelation which has Come*

*down to us and in that Which came down to
you; Our God and your
God Is One; and it is to Him We bow (in Islam).*

However, when Muhammad and his teachings were not
readily accepted, his whole outlook and attitude changed and this
became evident in his Qur'an writings concerning Jews and
Christians.

To Show the Bible as the Authority

*Surah 5:46-47 "And in their footsteps We sent
Jesus the son of Mary, confirming the Law that
had come before him: We sent him the Gospel:
Therein was guidance and light, and
confirmation of the Law that had come before
him: A guidance and an admonition to those
who fear Allah.
47 Let the People of the Gospel judge by what
Allah hath revealed therein. If any do fail to
judge by (the light of) what Allah hath revealed,
they are (no better than) those who rebel."*

Especially notice this next verse from the Qur'an. Remember
the argument of the Muslim is that God brought forth the Qur'an
because the Bible had become corrupted and was no longer valid.

*Surah 5:48 To thee We sent the Scripture in
truth, confirming the scripture that came before
it, and guarding it in safety: So judge between
them by what Allah hath revealed, and follow
not their vain desires, diverging from the Truth
that hath come to thee. To each among you have
We prescribed a Law and an Open way. If Allah
had so willed, he would have made you a single*

People, but (His Plan is) to test you in what He hath given you: So strive as in a race in all virtues. The goal of you all is to Allah; it is He that will show you the truth of the matters in which ye dispute;

The passage you just read said that the Qur'an was to confirm the Bible not replace it. It was also to guard the Bible and to keep it from being corrupted. According to the Qur'an itself and the teachings of Islam, the Qur'an has failed if the Bible has been corrupted.

Surah 5:68-69 Say: "O People of the Book! Ye have no ground to stand upon unless ye stand fast by the Law, the Gospel, and all the revelation that has come to you from your Lord." It is the revelation that cometh to thee from thy Lord, that increaseth in most of them their obstinate rebellion and blasphemy. But sorrow thou not over (these) people without Faith.
69 Those who believe (in the Qur'an), those who follow the Jewish (scriptures), and the Sabians and the Christians, --any who believe in Allah and the Last Day, and work righteousness, --on them shall be no fear, nor shall they grieve."

Surah 5:77 Say: "O People of the Book! Exceed not in your religion the bounds (of what is proper), trespassing beyond the truth, nor follow the vain desires of people who went wrong in times gone by, --who misled many, and stray (themselves) from the even way."

Surah 10:94 "If thou wert in doubt as to what

*We have revealed unto thee, then ask those who
have been reading the Book from before thee:
The Truth hath indeed come to thee from thy
Lord: So be in no wise of those in doubt."*

The above verse tells Muhammad that if he doubts what he is
being told he should go to the people that have been reading the
Book before him for confirmation of the truth. The Bible is the
only book to which the Qur'an can be referencing, and the Jews
and the Christians are the people to which it is referring.
Therefore, according to the Qur'an, the Muslim is to come to
Christians for truth from the Bible. Once again if the Bible were
corrupt, why would God send them to it for confirmation of truth?
Therefore, according to the Qur'an, the Bible is not corrupt, and it
is still the true authority.

*Surah 29:47 "And thus (it is) that We have sent
down the Book to thee. So the People of the
Book believe therein, as also do some of these
(Pagan Arabs): And none but Unbelievers reject
Our Signs."*

Muslims do not reject all of the New Testament as being
unauthentic. In fact they often use certain parts of it to show or
prove their beliefs that Jesus did not claim to be God. Any
passages from the Bible that will support their doctrines, they will
declare them to be accurate and authentic. On the other hand, if
the Bible does not support their doctrines, it will quickly and
arbitrarily be pronounced corrupted.

To Show That What Jesus Said, They Were to Obey

*Surah 5:78 Curses were pronounced on those
among the Children of Israel who rejected
Faith, by the tongue of David and of Jesus the*

195

son of Mary: Because they disobeyed and persisted in excesses.

Muslims rank Muhammad above Jesus as a prophet, but if they would examine the facts that the Qur'an has confirmed they could not do so. First, Jesus had a miraculous conception, second, Jesus lived a life full of miracles, and third, Jesus had a miraculous finish to his life on earth even from the view of Islam. According to Islam he did not die but was taken up of God. What other prophet had all three of these things (according to their Qur'an) laid to their account?

To Show Man Speaking In It

The whole first surah is a human prayer, in which God is addressed in the second and third persons. Islam's main argument against the Bible is that it is written by man, with man's styles of literary form. They claim that the Qur'an is written with God speaking in the first person.

Thus we have their claim that the Bible has been tampered with by man and has been rewritten to suite man. With well over 5,000 Greek manuscripts of the New Testament, it is safe to say that the New Testament is the most documented historical book in the world today. Islam cannot boast this of their Qur'an. The New Testament dates back to the first century as far as a completed copy. The Qur'an only dates back to the seventh century.

Chapter XV
ISLAM'S ROLE IN THE END TIMES

What does Islam's role in the end times mean to the true child of God? I believe it means that our home-going is soon. Islam is a major player in the end times. As I said earlier, everything that God does Satan attempts to counterfeit it. Satan's counterfeits are always corrupted and perverse trying to defile the things of God.

Almost all writers on prophecy have focused on Rome, the Catholic Church, and the Pope concerning end time prophecies. However, in more recent days many have begun to make a shift towards Islam as a major player in the last days. Islam was not considered or even noticed much until 9-11 took place. Then it seemed as though the religion of Islam sprang to the forefront almost overnight. The things that I am sharing with you are what I have been teaching our missionaries since January of 1996.

I believe that Satan used the Catholic Church as a diversion to keep Islam in the background until it was ready to be revealed. I mentioned earlier that it is now the largest religion in the world with nearly 1.9 billion followers. It already had taken the lead when its presence was revealed so strongly on 9-11, although many continued to say Christianity was the largest religion, trying to comfort us with that statement. The Trojan horse was already in place, even in our nation.

I have a video clip from the Larry King Show in 2011 on my computer that I have downloaded from the internet. It has a catholic priest on it praising Islam and Muhammad and saying that Catholics need to learn from this beautiful religion. Catholics have never given ground to other religions. They have been the persecutors of others that opposed them.

You may remember that shortly after Pope Benedict XVI became pope he made a statement about the violence of Islam. Muslims rioted around the world, and he responded back, "I am sorry if my words were misinterpreted." The Muslim world rose up in anger about his accusations, and he publicly began to recant his statements. He wanted no part of the conflict with the Muslim world. We have never before seen anything like this take place. We are seeing Islam coming to the forefront as a religion as never before.

Islam has not only become tolerated in the United States and the world, but it has become accepted.

I have been told that you can take a frog and place it in a pan of room temperature water. You can then set that pan on the stove and begin to slowly turn up the heat. They say that the frog will remain in that water as the heat is turned up until the frog is cooked. The reason this happens is because the frog becomes acclimated to the temperature, because it is gradual.

This illustration describes what has been taking place in the world and the religion of Islam. We have been slowly brainwashed and indoctrinated with the religion to the point that the world thinks it is okay, not realizing it is the destruction of everyone that is not a Muslim. There have been many factors involved in the acclimation, from TV shows, movies, news media, internet, and even the classroom. It has come from so many different directions that most people have not seen it coming.

In Public Schools

Almost immediately, after the planes hit the World Trade Center in New York, a push for a textbook began in the public schools. The textbook (*Across the Centuries*) was published earlier but had not gained popularity. There was even a second edition published in 1999. This textbook was a major step toward indoctrinating our youth in the religion of Islam.

The textbook is entitled *Across the Centuries* and is published by Houghton Mifflin. It is a social studies textbook for the seventh and eighth grades. You can go to their web site and download lesson plans, activities, and much more to see for yourself.

It is not the textbook used in every school, but it is in use in every state from reports that I have received. This textbook deals very little with Christianity, the church, or Judaism, but goes into great detail concerning Islam and its history.

The propagation of Islam takes on four forms within the pages of the textbook and these are presented as historical facts.

First, in the form of apologetics - everything Islamic is praised and every problem ignored. It tells how they were tolerant of those they conquered but nothing of the violence toward the Jews and those indifferent to their views.

Second, in the form of distortion – jihad, which literally means holy war, or sacred war is presented as a struggle to do one's best to resist temptation and overcome evil. It ignores the fact that Muslim women enjoy fewer rights than probably any other women in the world.

Third, in the form of identification as Muslims - students are given homework assignments that repeatedly involve mock-

199

Muslim exercises. Students are to assume the name of a Muslim patriarch for role-play. Assignments such as memorizing Qur'an passages, memorizing Islamic prayers, praying to Allah, and much more are assigned activities.

Fourth, in the form of piety - the textbook endorses key articles of Islamic faith. It informs students that Ramadan is holy, "because in this month Muhammad received his first revelation from Allah." It tells why the architecture of the mosque is so designed.

There is nothing of Jesus as the Son of God or the holocaust mentioned in the book, but Islam is exalted. The church is dealt with in chapter 11, acknowledging the power of the church in lesson 1. In lesson 3 of chapter 11, the crusades make the Christians out to be villains while defending Islam. Then in chapter 13, lessons 1 through 4 describe the decline of the church and its loss of power.

By role-playing or simulation the student is encouraged to learn about the history and culture of Islam and the Islamic world by, as they say, "becoming Muslims."

Some schools have reportedly hung large banners on or in front of the school buildings during these weeks of role-playing. These banners read, "There is one God, Allah, and Mohammed is his prophet."

Muslim beliefs are taught as facts in the public schools of our nation, thanks to the Houghton Mifflin textbook that accepted input from the Council of Islamic Education (CIE) which helped write the textbook. Later the Houghton Mifflin publisher cited that the Council of Islamic Education did not help write the text; they only reviewed it.

In Politics

In 1995, President Bill Clinton played a major role in the acceptance of Islam into both the schools and the school curriculum. President Clinton's "Religious Expression in Public Schools Guidelines" opened the doors for Islam in the classrooms of our nation. He met regularly with the director of the American Muslim Council who participated in the original drafts of the guidelines.

One of President Clinton's nominees, District Judge Phyllis Hamilton, approved the following prayer as a lesson for students to learn, "In the name of Allah, the Compassionate, the Merciful. Praise be to Allah, Lord of Creation, The Compassionate, the Merciful, King of Judgment-day! You alone we worship, and to You alone we pray for help, Guide us to the straight path."

The prayer is left to the discretion of the teacher but can be implemented if the teacher so desires.

"First Lady Hillary Rodham Clinton Hosted Muslims for Eid Al Fitr Celebration." This was the headline of the *Muslim Journal* on March 15, 1996. The article stated, "The acceptance of Al-Islam in America has reached to the highest office in America." This article appeared one year after her husband had given Muslims an open invitation through the textbooks to indoctrinate our children in the public schools.

Most people are not and may never be aware of what was taking place in the White House of the United States of America. Hillary Clinton is quoted throughout the article as praising, admiring, and exalting Islam as a religion that would help our nation. The following are quotes from the *Muslim Journal* made by Hillary Clinton.

"As the fastest growing religion in the country, Islam will only continue to enrich our people and our society. And a greater understanding of the tenets of Islam in our national consciousness will help build strength and resilience as a nation. That is why the President and I believe this is such an historic – and overdue occasion"

"Like many Americans, I have only recently gained a full appreciation of Islam. When I was growing up, there were no courses in Islamic history in my schools, and the Qur'an was not on too many bookshelves in American households. Fortunately that has changed as I know from my own family experience."

"The Qur'an has touched and enlightened billions, including my own family. And as I learn more about Islam and about all the great religions, I am struck by the remarkable similarities among them."

The article also showed pictures of Hillary Clinton receiving a Qur'an from Chaplain Abdul Rasheed Muhammad of Ft. Bragg, N.C., the first Islamic Chaplain to serve in the United States military.

President George W. Bush came into office; and, unless it was done behind the scenes, he made no attempt to undo what the former President Bill Clinton did in our schools' curriculum.

In April 2005, President Bush and Prime Minister Ariel Sharon of Israel met in disagreement about giving West Bank territory to the Palestinians. President Bush sided against Israel. Secretary Condoleezza Rice also pushed Israel in giving up borders in July 2007.

President Bush also favored a Palestinian state and Israel giving up territory. January 10, 2008, headlines were: "US President George W. Bush has said Israel must end its occupation of some Arab land to enable the creation of a viable Palestinian State."

During the campaign for the 2008 Presidential elections Senator Barack Hussein Obama pledged to cut military spending, and to downsize our military and our nuclear arsenal. He mocked the Bible and belittled Christianity saying that folks have not been reading their Bibles. He was a member of Jeremiah Wright's church that embraced Louis Farrakhan (Leader of the Nation of Islam) and Pastor Wright had him in the pulpit on more than one occasion. Farrakhan even praised Senator Barack Hussein Obama as being the savior. Senator Barack Obama even admitted in an interview that Senator John McCain never once questioned his Muslim faith. In spite of all these things he was still elected President.

Once elected President, he received calls from Muslim countries congratulating him on his victory. Note, no other President has been that accepted and praised by Muslim leaders around the world. Why would he be so accepted by Muslim leaders around the world?

Could it be because in 2006 Senator Barack Hussein Obama went to Kenya and campaigned for Raila Odinga (Opposition Leader in Kenya that signed a "Shariah pact" with Muslims)? (Raila Odinga also claims to be President Obama's relation). This same Raila Odinga instigated the violence that took the lives of over 1,500 people in post-election violence when he lost. Many of those killed were in churches that were set on fire, and as they ran out they were slaughtered with machetes.

Since President Barack Hussein Obama's election, on many occasions, he has quoted from the Qur'an (with emphasis and feeling, not like his mocking of the Bible), embraced Islam as a great religion, and even boasted of coming from a long line of

Muslims on his father's side of the family. His father was a Muslim from the Luo tribe in Kenya. His family members are still Muslims and claim him to be as well.

In 2012 the Prime Minister of Israel, Benjamin Netanyahu, confronted him about throwing Israel under the bus. President Obama made attempts to smooth things over, but his true character is coming out. He is quoted as saying, "America will never be at war with Islam." He has pushed our nation to the brink of bankruptcy with bailouts and spending. He has allowed General Motors to move the majority of its operations to China after General Motors received a huge bailout, without repaying the taxpayers' dollars that bailed them out. He has been the first President ever to bow before a Muslim leader, submitting to their authority.

I love my country dearly, but this world is not my home as the song says. As much as I love my country, I know that America has to go down as a nation. Most prophetic scholars have always taught that America is destroyed, and that is why you cannot find America mentioned during the tribulation.

Well, they are right in that America is not mentioned during the tribulation period. However, it is not because it has been destroyed or annihilated, but it is because it has been brought down to a stature of no importance. America will continue to exist but only as a country with little power and little influence on the rest of the world. It will no longer be an economic power or a military power. We are almost there even as I write this book.

Islam has invaded our country from within. It is in our military and has been evidenced on several occasions:

- The American soldier that threw the grenade into the tent of American officers

204

in the early part of the Iraq War was also a Muslim.

- The Soldier on Ft. Hood Army Base that shot and killed several other soldiers in 2011 was a Muslim.

Islam has also invaded our political offices. They have been elected to school boards, state offices, and federal positions. They hold positions in the White House.

Our nation is all but removed from power, and as Christians we know that God is able to deliver. However, I also know that it is God that sets up and takes down rulers. With that said, God must have put President Obama in the position for a reason. Could it be that he is the chosen forerunner to prepare for the antichrist. Has he been put here to remove our nation from its place of power?

He was an amateur with no experience at all, arrogant and proud, boastful, and cast forth by his party. He has been exalted to the highest political office in our nation. Now our nation is heading in a downward spiral.

Isaiah 14:12-16 How art thou fallen from heaven, O Lucifer, son of the morning! how art thou cut down to the ground, which didst weaken the nations!
13 For thou hast said in thine heart, I will ascend into heaven, I will exalt my throne above the stars of God: I will sit also upon the mount of the congregation, in the sides of the north:
14 I will ascend above the heights of the clouds; I will be like the most High.
15 Yet thou shalt be brought down to hell, to the

sides of the pit.
16 They that see thee shall narrowly look upon
thee, and *consider thee,* saying, Is *this the man*
that made the earth to tremble, that did shake
kingdoms;

Luke 10:18 And he said unto them, I beheld
Satan as lightning fall from heaven.

Note two Hebrew words, one is for our English word lightning, and the other is for our English word heights. In the previous passages Satan wanted to ascend and exalt his throne above the heights. Also, he was cast down as lightning in Luke 10:18.

The *Strong's Exhaustive Concordance* gives the following definitions of the two words "lightning" and "heights."

01300 baraq baw-rawk'; from 01299; lightning; by analogy, a gleam; concretely, a flashing sword: - bright, glitter(ing sword), lightning.

01116 bamah bam-maw'; from an unused root (meaning to be high); an elevation: - height, high place, wave.

I am just giving you the definitions from the concordance; you draw your own conclusion. I have drawn mine; as I stated earlier, the antichrist needs a forerunner to prepare the way.

During my devotions recently I had another verse stand out which seemed very interesting concerning our present day events. Multitudes went out to see the forerunner of Christ, and to hear what this man had to say.

Ezekiel 20:29 Then I said unto them, What is the high place whereunto ye go? And the name thereof is called Bamah unto this day.

In November 2006, Keith Ellison was the first Muslim elected to congress in Minnesota and sworn in with a Qur'an that was owned by former President Thomas Jefferson.

As long as America is running to the aid of nations around the world and trying to answer the problems of the world, the antichrist will not be revealed. The antichrist when revealed will be the one with the answers to bring about what seems to be peace. Of course it will be a false peace, and will only last for three and one half years.

We know that the antichrist will not be revealed until the church is raptured out of this world. So, given the state of our nation, and the things that are falling into place, I believe that we are very close to hearing that trumpet sound.

Look at the number of Muslim nations that have lost their leaders and are looking for a leader. The Muslim world is looking for Muhammad al-Mahdi to return to set up his rule. Even Ahmadinejad the Iranian leader that hates the Jews and wants to annihilate them is looking for the return of the twelfth imam. He also believes he is to be preparing for his imminent return. Now, they do not see him as the antichrist, but they are looking for one to come and rule the world.

Christians know that the only one who is going to establish a one-world religion and a one-world government before Christ establishes His Millennial Kingdom will be the antichrist. I believe with all of my heart that our time is quickly running out to reach the lost for Christ. End times are upon us, and Islam is rapidly rising to the forefront around the world.

In Public News Media

March 23, 2007, Brit Hume of Fox News covered a story titled, "No Divorce Cites Koran." The article read as follows:

A female judge in Germany cited the Koran in her refusal to allow a Muslim woman permission to file for an immediate divorce over abuse by her husband, saying that the Koran allows a man to beat his wife. The woman in question said her husband not only beat her but also threatened to kill her.

German's were outraged by the judge's decision. Top newspaper headlines read: "Where are we living? Woman judge allows beating in marriage and invokes the Koran." And a government official said, "When the Koran takes precedence over the German Basic Law, then I can only say: Goodnight to Germany."

In the "Online Human Events," *The National Conservative Weekly*, Robert Spencer writes the following, which was posted September 16, 2004.

How quickly is Europe being Islamized? Sweden's third-largest city, Malmo, according to the Swedish Aftonbladet, has become an outpost of the Middle East in Scandinavia: "The police now publicly admit what many Scandinavians have known for a long time: They no longer control the situation in the nation's third-largest city. It is effectively ruled by violent gangs of Muslim immigrants."

The Nordgardsskolen in Aarhus, Denmark, has become the first Dane-free school. The students now come entirely from Demark's fastest growing constituency - Muslim immigrants. Also in Denmark, the Qur'an is now required reading for all upper-secondary school students.

Robert Spencer goes on to say that Europe began thirty years ago to travel down a path of appeasement, accommodation, and cultural abdication before Islam in pursuit of short-sighted political and economic benefits.

A headline in the <u>Indianapolis Star</u> written by Cathy Lynn Grossman, January 27, 2011 reads:

Study: Muslims' numbers rising. Estimates say group will grow to more than 25% of world's population in a study released today. The number of U.S. Muslims will double. Muslim numbers have been growing at a faster rate than all other groups combined.

Sean Hannity of Fox News spoke on his program one night with a man that claimed to be a former jihadist. The question was asked, "Do the Muslims hate the Jews so much that they would be willing to kill thousands or millions of their own people to destroy the Jews?" The man did not even hesitate when he said in a heartbeat, "most definitely." Jerusalem is not the Muslim's holy city; it is the holy city of the Jews. The Muslims are there to keep the Jews from totally occupying it. To destroy it would not bother the Muslims at all.

Another question was asked. What are Al Qaeda, the Taliban, Hamas, and these other extremist groups? The man answered, "They are like cheerleaders, trying to rally the Muslim world together."

The Muslim world is still divided to a great degree, even fighting against one another. However, when they can focus on a common enemy that they hate more than each other, they will unite. This is the goal of these groups. This is why former President George W. Bush declared war on terror and not Islam. You better believe Islam is the root of it. Their Qur'an teaches and endorses their hatred and violence towards all non-Muslims. Their Qur'an says, "Never will it be accepted other than Islam." They are not tolerant of you and me.

There is also a video on the internet that is very interesting in showing the growth and dominance of Islam. Open your web browser and type in your search engine, Muslim Demographics. It is only a few years old, but it is already outdated in its predictions. However, it still gets the point across about the growth, expansion, and dominance of the religion of Islam. It clearly shows the global movement of the religion.

Global domination is the objective of the leaders of this religion that has so rapidly come to the forefront in recent years. Muslims are not and will not be content until they have total control, and there's but one religion - "Islam."

Chapter XVI
ISLAM'S ROLE IN TRIBULATION TIMES

As we have seen the growth and expansion of this religion, we have also seen its intolerance for other religions. Yet, for it to come to the forefront as it has and will, something is going to have to take place to make this possible. Other religions are not likely to just lie down and give place to this religion.

As a Christian I will and do take a stand for my Savior, and I know that other true Christians will as well. This will allow Islam as a religion to advance only so far. We have God on our side.

> *Romans 8:31 What shall we then say to these things? If God be for us, who can be against us?*

However, the day is rapidly approaching, and I believe it is even at hand when God is going to call us out. We often refer to this as the Rapture of the Church.

> *1 Thessalonians 5:1-11 But of the times and the seasons, brethren, ye have no need that I write unto you.*
>
> *2 For yourselves know perfectly that the day of the Lord so cometh as a thief in the night.*
>
> *3 For when they shall say, Peace and safety; then sudden destruction cometh upon them, as travail upon a woman with child; and they shall not escape.*
>
> *4 But ye, brethren, are not in darkness, that that day*

should overtake you as a thief.
5 Ye are all the children of light, and the children of the day: we are not of the night, nor of darkness.
6 Therefore let us not sleep, as do others; but let us watch and be sober.
7 For they that sleep sleep in the night; and they that be drunken are drunken in the night.
8 But let us, who are of the day, be sober, putting on the breastplate of faith and love; and for an helmet, the hope of salvation.
9 For God hath not appointed us to wrath, but to obtain salvation by our Lord Jesus Christ,
10 Who died for us, that, whether we wake or sleep, we should live together with him.
11 Wherefore comfort yourselves together, and edify one another, even as also ye do.

Our home going is so very close, and I believe that even more than ever as I watch the world events taking place. The fact that we are nearing our home going is easily seen as I consider the things involving Islam. God has made it very plain that He does not want us to be ignorant.

I Thessalonians 4:13-18 But I would not have you to be ignorant, brethren, concerning them which are asleep, that ye sorrow not, even as others which have no hope.
14 For if we believe that Jesus died and rose again, even so them also which sleep in Jesus will God bring with him.
15 For this we say unto you by the word of the Lord, that we which are alive and remain unto the coming of the Lord shall not prevent them which are asleep.

16 For the Lord himself shall descend from heaven with a shout, with the voice of the archangel, and with the trump of God: and the dead in Christ shall rise first:
17 Then we which are alive and remain shall be caught up together with them in the clouds, to meet the Lord in the air: and so shall we ever be with the Lord.
18 Wherefore comfort one another with these words.

When the rapture takes place, there will be no Christians left anywhere on the earth. There will be no resistance from a Christian standpoint. This will be the beginning of the "Tribulation Period."

II Thessalonians 2:2-12 Now we beseech you, brethren, by the coming of our Lord Jesus Christ, and by our gathering together unto him,

2 That ye be not soon shaken in mind, or be troubled, neither by spirit, nor by word, nor by letter as from us, as that the day of Christ is at hand.

3 Let no man deceive you by any means: for that day shall not come, except there come a falling away first, and that man of sin be revealed, the son of perdition;

4 Who opposeth and exalteth himself above all that is called God, or that is worshipped; so that he as God sitteth in the temple of God, shewing himself that he is God.

5 Remember ye not, that, when I was yet with you, I told you these things?

6 And now ye know what withholdeth that he might be revealed in his time.

213

7 For the mystery of iniquity doth already work: only he who now letteth will let, until he be taken out of the way.
8 And then shall that Wicked be revealed, whom the Lord shall consume with the spirit of his mouth, and shall destroy with the brightness of his coming:
9 Even him, whose coming is after the working of Satan with all power and signs and lying wonders,
10 And with all deceivableness of unrighteousness in them that perish; because they received not the love of the truth, that they might be saved.
11 And for this cause God shall send them strong delusion, that they should believe a lie:
12 That they all might be damned who believed not the truth, but had pleasure in unrighteousness.

When we are removed, the son of perdition will be revealed. Therefore, he must already be alive before our being called out, and will have been for a number of years. He will come on the scene as a man of wisdom with all the right answers.

The Antichrist Making His Debut

Imagine with me the following scene for the antichrist to make his appearance. Either just before or soon after the trumpet sounds and the rapture of the church happens, a blast that destroys the mosque on the Temple Mount takes place. Thousands or even millions are killed. Included in the mass numbers are Jews, Muslims, Catholics and Christians. It will be the perfect scene for the antichrist to make his appearance and begin his campaign of peace. Of course it is a false peace, but that will not be seen for three and one half years when the great tribulation will begin. He will announce that everyone has suffered great loss, and the loss will have everyone in a frame of mind to stop their warring and come together in their grief, trying to find comfort.

His efforts to build peace will cause a combined effort to build a temple where all can worship together. Construction will begin and all will seem to be going well until it is time to dedicate the temple. Then as the sacrifice is made upon the altar, the Jews will see who he really is. It will not be a swine as in Daniel, for a Muslim would not touch that. Instead, it will be a camel, which is an unclean beast to the Jews, but it is what Muslims sacrifice. What Daniel is prophesying to take place is the desecration of the altar by an unclean sacrifice. This is the abomination of desolation spoken of in Matthew 24.

> *Matthew 24:15-21 When ye therefore shall see the abomination of desolation, spoken of by Daniel the prophet, stand in the holy place, (whoso readeth, let him understand:)*
> *16 Then let them which be in Judaea flee into the mountains:*
> *17 Let him which is on the housetop not come down to take any thing out of his house:*
> *18 Neither let him which is in the field return back to take his clothes.*
> *19 And woe unto them that are with child, and to them that give suck in those days!*
> *20 But pray ye that your flight be not in the winter, neither on the sabbath day:*
> *21 For then shall be great tribulation, such as was not since the beginning of the world to this time, no, nor ever shall be.*

Now, there is do doubt who this man is that brought this unity and seeming peace. He has now revealed his true identity, and now attempts to utterly destroy the Jews once and for all.

You may ask, "Why would they come together and build a temple?" Do you remember when the New York World Trade

215

Center was destroyed? Do you remember how the sympathy of the world poured out to the United States for a while? There were 2,977 victims in the 9-11 attacks on the World Trade Center, and that was a tremendous loss. However, can you imagine the scene there in Jerusalem following the devastation of an event that would level the mosque on the Temple Mount and take thousands or even millions of lives? Miraculously, there appears on the scene a man that can say brethren we have suffered enough. Let us come together in peace - "The antichrist."

It will only take a moment for the Muslims to resume their hatred for the Jews when this leader reveals his true character. The Jews will flee for their lives, and the Great Tribulation will have begun. Three and one half years of tribulation worse than the world has ever seen will begin. This will last until Christ sets His foot upon the earth and subdues His enemies and establishes His Millennial Kingdom.

Some Things That Satan Has Copied
God chose to bring the promised seed out of Abraham. God brought forth Isaac and according to God's Word He established that covenant in the book of Genesis; Satan brought forth Ishmael through a handmaid named Hagar.

God brought forth twelve tribes from Isaac; now Satan brings forth twelve princes from Ishmael.

God brought His Only Begotten Son through one of His twelve tribes born of a virgin: Satan will bring forth his son through one of his twelve princes but not through a virgin birth.

God's Son ministered three and one half years living a spotless example of a sinless life and showed the world who He really was as He laid down His life for the world. Christ did this demonstrating a love that is unmatched, unequaled, and undeserved by all mankind. Satan's son will minister three and one half years of false peace (first half of the tribulation) and will then show the world who he really is and attempt to destroy the Jews once and for all (The Great Tribulation, the last three and one half years). He will demonstrate a hatred that is unmatched and unequaled against all mankind and against God.

The whole focus of tribulation times is upon Jerusalem where the antichrist will be seated. The focus is not Rome, but Jerusalem, which I believe is the city on seven hills spoken of in Daniel. Everyone has always believed Daniel was speaking of Rome because of Titus coming in and destroying Jerusalem in A.D. 70. However, we seem to forget the Ottoman Turks (Muslims) coming in hundreds of years later and destroying Jerusalem, and they have occupied at least portions of the city and controlled the Temple Mount ever since.

You can go on the internet and type in: "City on seven hills," and see that there are several cities that are listed. Istanbul, Turkey is one of the cities listed, which was the capital or seat of Islam for several years. Jerusalem is also listed and there are even maps showing the names of the seven hills. After all, Jerusalem is where the antichrist will establish his throne and rule. Jerusalem will be the focal point of the entire world during that time.

I think we need to remember that no one has ever wanted the Jew destroyed more than the descendants of Ishmael. Even Hitler during World War II joined forces with Muslims against the Jews in an effort to destroy them. He was a white supremacist, but he was willing to join forces with someone that hated the Jews as much he did. The descendants of Ishmael have never gotten over the feeling that they were robbed of their birthright when Isaac was chosen instead Ishmael. They not only hate the Jews, but also anyone that sympathizes with them.

Genesis 12:3 And I will bless them that bless thee, and curse him that curseth thee: and in thee shall all families of the earth be blessed.

Acts 5:29 Then Peter and the other apostles answered and said, We ought to obey God rather than men.

I believe we ought to just obey God and bless them (the Jew) rather than obey the Muslim and hate the Jew.

Luke 21:25-28 And there shall be signs in the sun, and in the moon, and in the stars; and upon the earth distress of nations, with perplexity; the sea and the waves roaring;
26 Men's hearts failing them for fear, and for looking after those things which are coming on the earth: for the powers of heaven shall be shaken.
27 And then shall they see the Son of man coming in a cloud with power and great glory.
28 And when these things begin to come to pass, then look up, and lift up your heads; for your redemption draweth nigh.

This is not to alarm us but to show that home-going for the redeemed is at hand. The songwriter reminds us, "Soon We Shall See Jesus."

If we are going to do a work for the Lord, we had better get busy. Our time is short. I know that people have said that for many years, even generations, but never has the world been in the shape it is right now. Look at the number of countries needing leaders, economic failure in so many countries at the same time, wars, and rumors of war.

Lately, I have heard preachers saying, "It may be even hundreds of years till His return." "Don't you think that during the Civil War people thought surely this is the end?"

Maybe I am wrong, but that to me sounds like scoffing.

II Peter 3:1-14 This second epistle, beloved, I now write unto you; in both which I stir up your pure minds by way of remembrance:
2 That ye may be mindful of the words which were spoken before by the holy prophets, and of the commandment of us the apostles of the Lord and Saviour:
3 Knowing this first, that there shall come in the last days scoffers, walking after their own lusts,
4 And saying, Where is the promise of his coming? for since the fathers fell asleep, all things continue as they were from the beginning of the creation.
5 For this they willingly are ignorant of, that by the word of God the heavens were of old, and the earth standing out of the water and in the water:
6 Whereby the world that then was, being overflowed with water, perished:
7 But the heavens and the earth, which are now, by the same word are kept in store, reserved unto fire against the day of judgment and perdition of ungodly men.
8 But, beloved, be not ignorant of this one thing, that one day is with the Lord as a thousand years, and a thousand years as one day.
9 The Lord is not slack concerning his promise, as some men count slackness; but is longsuffering to us-ward, not willing that any should perish, but that all should come to repentance.

10 But the day of the Lord will come as a thief in the night; in the which the heavens shall pass away with a great noise, and the elements shall melt with fervent heat, the earth also and the works that are therein shall be burned up.

11 Seeing then that all these things shall be dissolved, what manner of persons ought ye to be in all holy conversation and godliness,

12 Looking for and hasting unto the coming of the day of God, wherein the heavens being on fire shall be dissolved, and the elements shall melt with fervent heat?

13 Nevertheless we, according to his promise, look for new heavens and a new earth, wherein dwelleth righteousness.

14 Wherefore, beloved, seeing that ye look for such things, be diligent that ye may be found of him in peace, without spot, and blameless.

Unbelief is crippling our churches today. Let me explain what I mean. If the members of our churches truly believed that our time was short, there would be a much different lifestyle being displayed, dedication evidenced, service performed unto the Lord, and more of a burden for the lost shown.

Unbelief is a wicked, vile, ungodly testimony for any child of God. We will testify to the things that we believe concerning the Word of God, but we are not so quick to testify of the things we do not believe.

However, watch a person's actions and their lifestyle; their beliefs come to life in how they live. Most church members today are living in unbelief concerning the Lord's return. Either scoffing or just not really believing He is coming back or at least not any time soon.

Hebrews 3:12 Take heed, brethren, lest there be in any of you an evil heart of unbelief, in departing from the living God.

Matthew 24:48 But and if that evil servant shall say in his heart, My lord delayeth his coming;

Isaiah 51:6 Lift up your eyes to the heavens, and look upon the earth beneath: for the heavens shall vanish away like smoke, and the earth shall wax old like a garment, and they that dwell therein shall die in like manner: but my salvation shall be for ever, and my righteousness shall not be abolished.

Luke 21:28 And when these things begin to come to pass, then look up, and lift up your heads; for your redemption draweth nigh.

Psalms 121:1 I will lift up mine eyes unto the hills, from whence cometh my help.

I Thessalonians 5:2 For yourselves know perfectly that the day of the Lord so cometh as a thief in the night.
I Thessalonians 5:4 But ye, brethren, are not in darkness, that that day should overtake you as a thief.

Revelation 3:3 Remember therefore how thou hast received and heard, and hold fast, and repent. If therefore thou shalt not watch, I will come on thee as a thief, and thou shalt not know what hour I will come upon thee.

Revelation 16:15 Behold, I come as a thief. Blessed is he that watcheth, and keepeth his garments, lest he walk naked, and they see his shame.

Revelation 16:7 And I heard another out of the altar say, Even so, Lord God Almighty, true and righteous are thy judgments.

Revelation 22:20 He which testifieth these things saith, Surely I come quickly. **Amen. Even so, come, Lord Jesus.**

Bibliography

Across the Centuries Social Studies Textbook, Houghton Mifflin, 2001

Akridge, Professor Colin P., Why I cannot be a Black Muslim,

Ali, Abdullah Yusuf, The Holy Qur'an, Amana Corporation, 1993

Ali, Abdullah Yusuf, Koran translation

Baagil, H.M., Christian Muslim Dialogue, January 1984

Caner, Ergun Mehmet and Caner, Emir Fethi, Unveiling Islam, Kregel Publishers, 2002

El, R. Love, Oral Statements and Prophesies of Prophet Noble Drew Ali, 1988

Encyclopedia Britannica

Geisler, Norman L. & Abdul Saleeb, Answering Islam, Baker Books, May 1994

Gurganus, Gene, Perils of Islam, Truth Publishers, 2004

King James Bible

Martin, Walter, Kingdom of the Cults, Bethany House Publishers, 2003

Mohammed, Moulana, Siddiqui, Abdul-Aleem, Elementary Teachings of Islam, Kazi Publications, 1994

Morey, Robert, The Islamic Invasion, Chick Publications

Muslim Journal, March 1996

Muslim Journal May 30, 2008

Online Human Events, National Conservative Weekly

Poole, Matthew, Matthew Poole's Commentary, MacDonald Publishers

Research and Education Foundation

The Custodian of The Two Holy Mosques King Fahd Complex

The Presidency of Islamic Researches, IFTA, The Holy Qur'an,

World Book Encyclopedia
Wikipedia Encyclopedia
http://www.absoluteastronomy.com/topics/Black_Stone
http://www.catholic-hierarchy.org/country/sc1.html
https://www.cia.gov/library/publications/cia-maps-
 publications/index.html
https://www.cia.gov/library/publications/the-world-
 factbook/maps/maptemplate_xx.html
https://www.cia.gov/library/publications/the-world-
www.cnn.com
http://www.danielpipes.org/118/think-like-a-muslim-urges-across-
 the-centuries
http://www.danielpipes.org/blog/2003/12/courts-okay-to-
 proselytize-for-islam-in
www.FoxNews.com
www.msnbc.com
http://www.muhammadspeaks.com/Peddler.html
http://www.religioustolerance.org/worldrel.htm
http://en.wikipedia.org/wiki/Black_Stone